Old Love Skin:

Voices from Conteporary Africa

This is an uncorrected proof

Old Love Skin:
Voices from Conteporary Africa

First Edition

Mukana Press
1200 Franklin Mall, Box 459,
Santa Clara, CA, 95052

This book is a work of fiction. References to historical events or real people and places are used fictitiously. Other names, events, characters, and places are products of the author's imagination, and any resemblance to actual events or places or persons, living or dead, is entirely coincidental.

Copyright © 2022 by poets

All rights reserved, including the right to reproduce this book or portions of this book in any form whatsoever, without the prior written permission of the copyright owner.

Published 2022

Manufactured in the United States of America
25 24 23 22 21 20 19 18 17   1 2 3 4 5

Library of Congress Control Number: 202294165

ISBN 9780578397153 (paperback)
ISBN 9798218029579 (Ebook)

Contents

Foreword *1*

Alvin Kathemb
'Little Black Boy' 3
'First And Forever' 5
'contingencies' 7

Henneh Kyereh Kwaku
 Gaana & Other Poems
playing god in old love skin 9
The Magician 10
Gaana 11

Gabrial Awuah Mainoo
Seven Shapes of God 12
Dream boy 13
A Black Skin Breaks Away from Hell 14

Ruvimbo Chido Chikanda (RUBZI)
Hey Mr. Paradox 15
Power Lenses 17
Bipolar Bladder 18

Christine Coates
 Threnody for a Queen in Four Parts – an Opera
2. The Girl 19
4. The Collapsed Mother..................................20

Kwaku Dade
To Aluah I..21
To Aluah II...23
Building Beauty...25

Jeremy T. Karn
   Portrait of a Liberian's Boy & Other Poems
Portrait of a Liberian's Boy...................................27
Sickle Cell Anaemia..29
The Making of Grief..30

Phodiso Modirwa
Another Dirge To Fill The Space Left Behind 31
Talking To My Mother About My Job (After Henneh Kyereh Kwaku)..33
Cento: Investigating Lonely....................................34

Taofeek Ayeyemi
Three Haibun Twist of Fate 36
Per Diem 37
Colour by Colour, Repainting my Dreams 38

Bryan Obinna Joseph Okwesili
Preacher Man Knows My Name 40
My Prayers Do Not Promise Me Heaven..................42
He Hatched Into a Howl.......................................43

Amirah Al Wassif
Human Tragedy 45
Diaries from jail...47
Hallucinations...48

Prince Rayanne Chidzvondo
The Stink 49
Allegedly 50
Days of July..51

Londeka Mduli
The Sky Has Robbers 53
Pigeon Houses..54
Immigration...55

Richard Mbuthia
Wistful Wisps 56
Edible Bubbles 58
Crumbs of Life...59

Timothy Fab-Eme
Ecocide in the Wake of Discovery and Dreams 60
We're Sick Now and Earth's Healing Real
Fast Spring 61
Echoing Loss as a Prelude to the Opera of
Bad Regimes...62

Nebeolisa Okwudili
The Making of Widows 63
Beggars...64
A Myth in Two Parts 66

Leroy Mtulisi Ndlovu
The Minister of (Good) Will 68
A Shopping Expedition During Lockdown..................69
A Looter Contiua 70

Pusetso Lame
Botswana 71
Thoughts..72
Dear death 74

Nsah Mala
Forbidden 76
Sometimes I Wonder..77
Cloudy Day..79

Isaac Kwaliba
The Art of Self Destruction 83
deaf-blind...85
It Is What It Is...87

Nehemiah Omukhonya
Shall We Live! 88
Shame 89

Ann Pendo
No 90
A Night...91
That's my mother 92

Eratso E. Noni
Song Of The Beauty 93
Africa, My Africa 95
The Sleeping Bees...97

Energy Mavaza
Behind My Brows 99
Run Run Girl!...101
Harvest of Thorns 102

Aisha Naise Ahmad
The Pure Test 103
You're My Catalyst..104
Unforgettable human 106

Carolyne M. Acen (Afroetry MA)
50 YEARS LATER..107
The Gospel According To Colonialism 110
Dark Skin Blues 112

Tryphena Yeboah
Mama 114
Coping Mechanism...116

Ronald K. Ssekajja
Convulsions 118
Shadow Hunters of My Joy 119
Flickering Moon..121

Jeresi Katusiime
Mother's Pride 122
For The Child Who Was Never Made 124
Do Not Tell My Husband 126

Carla-Ann Makumbe
Awaiting You 128
As she Is 129
We Are 132

Jasper Harry Sabuni
Does It? 134
If I Die Today..137
Silence..138

Nicole Natsai Chimanikire
It's Raining Today 139
Emotionally Numb 141
She came out of the sand of time 143

Justine Nagundi
The Sulking Son 145
The Eternal Noon 146
Lessons in Womanhood 147

Fungai Gwen Makuyana
In the Shadows 148
I loves you, Porgy..149
How They Made Her 150

Elizabeth Kayongwe Lukoma
Lies He Told 152
Redeem 154
Today Was..156

Emestina Edem Azah
Chestgrow Things 158
Help Me Sound Like Heaven Or It's Stairway So I Can
Be Close To You 160
States Of Matter; a Human Being Can Be Transmuted
When They Are Suffering and Still Exist....................162

Tatiana Natalie Kondo (banshee)
Enough 164
Salt..165
Drowning..166

Oppong Clifford Benjamin
Everything Ends at Where Everything Starts 167
The Building is in the Reconstruction 169
Choosing Colours for Destiny.....................................170

Billyhadiat Taofeeqoh Adeola
Paradise In Between My Thighs 171
Honeymoon Blues...173
This is Not Love 174

Nnane Ntube
Magical Pen 175
Nothing Like A Kiss 176
The Wait 177

Philani Amadeus Nyoni
  Three Sonnets
LXXIV 178
CLI 179
CCLV 180

Hauwa Shaffii Nunu
Fault Lines 181
Prayer..182
Prayers 184

Esnala Banda
Inception 185
Her Story - Flowers 187
Future Love Letters 189

Zziwa Zinbala
I Meant, He Is Gay Not Gay....................................191
For Richer, for Richer...194
Deep seated 196

Sihle Ntuli
Salvation 197
God of Small Things 199
The Saga (Concerning the Morning Call for Prayers)200

Gerry Sikazwe
Roots 202
Worn Boldly and Gratefully 204
Single Tick 205

Xitha Makgeta
P.O Box 16371 206
Truth Is In The Vomit. 207
It Is Blue In Harare 208

Ayouba Toure
A Song To The Fishes My Net Couldn't Hold 209
Because We Are Made Up of Water..........................210
Liberia..212

Sarpong Osei Asamoah
A Boy Made Of Lines 213
The Rain & I...214
Afrobeat 215

Caroline Anande Uliwa
Her Tabia (Habit) 216
Meeting Lonely...217
Fast Phrases 218

Adjei Agyei Baah
 3 Senryū
Endtime Sermon 220
Parting Through The Stars...221
Elec(sanc)tions 222

Acknowledgements..223
Contributors Biographical Notes................................226

Foreword

*you, god – have given
the crow the wind
& here is the crow flying against
the gift & not gliding with it –
you say take a bit more of white
& give me some black
--- Henneh Kyereh Kwaku*

How do you play god in skin that is not of your own making? How do you stay visible in a space that threatens to unmake you, and render you invisible? How do you speak the unspeakable? How do you amplify the dialects of your dialogue through (a) language that speaks everything against you? Old Love Skin is not an anthology of expressly love poems, or at least love as defined in the 'pure' romantic sense, it is of a love much deeper, much more ancient yet so urgent, a love that is passionate as it is resistant, and innovative. A love of grappling, a love of taking up space, a love of beauty, a love of finding, a love of words, images, sound and a love of the creative passion. Old Love Skin is an explosion of language marrying form, marrying content.

The most eternal of questions has been, what is it exactly that poets actually do? Over time, space and the ever changing ages, poets have been met with mixed feelings and reactions, they've been praised for their appreciation of beauty, their ability to put into words feelings or at least their attempts at doing so, they've been called lazy, they've been viewed as wise, witty and inventive, they've also been looked at as eccentric. Being a poet is as much an honour as it is a curse, and being a poet, writing and living on the African continent is no exception, if anything it is actually an act of resistance as it is an expression of the creative passions. Africa has a rich history of poetry as practised orally through its griots and praise singers, poetry has been used over the centuries as a carrier of history, values, as a way to teach, to invent and to entertain among other things; however, poetry meant to for the page hasn't been as celebrated. Africa has celebrated its novelists, essayists and short writers more that it has its poets, poets have been left to steal the little bits of limelight and praise. That has partly been a result of the idea that poetry (written) is a high art which is meant to be indulged by a select few, also compounded by Africa's liberation history against colonialism, in which writing became an active act of both resistance and liberation, poetry was looked as at best articulating a private voice, and thus could not carry the larger version of the liberation agenda.

Old Love Skin is an offering of possibilities; where radical imagination meets the sheer unrelenting power of creativity, here poets play god with language, form, images and voice, in a battle of reinvention, in ways that are humorous, urgent, striking, sometimes deep and contemplative. Here poets remind us what it is to be alive, what is it to be given the world and not knowing what to do with it, how different and not so difference we are. In here lies beauty, hope, fear, anger, resilience, love, redemption. Here poets remind us that poetry is powerful, is it cathartic and most importantly is far from being a dying art.

Nyashadzashe Chikumbu
Somewhere in Harare, Zimbabwe
2022

Alvin Kathemb

'Little Black Boy'

little black boy,
you are lovely,
you have never doubted that.
not even while playing with your
little white toys
and reading your
snow-white stories
out of little lily-white Ladybird books.
you love your
white music—
little white boys screaming into microphones;
and your white movies:
nerdy white boy Neo;
doing his Superman thing,
saving us all;
white Tom cruising
through impossible missions,
or mastering Kenjutsu in a winter;
suave white spies dying another day,
leaving you shaken,
and stirred.
but you are African,
you are black,
growing up in a world reverberating
with white voices.
No wonder
you feel uneasy
when you remember, when you realise

that you didn't even know
that you are African,
you are black,
until they told you.

'First And Forever'

I treat myself
gently, so gently.
I am patient with this fumbling body,
with this bungling mind.
I am, after all, only a child
forced into playing at being a grown-up.
I do not like this game.
I have been turned out into the world,
asked to forage and fend for myself.
I, a child,
only thirty years old,
expected to feed and clothe and maintain
this fumbling body, this bungling mind.
I am even—horror of horrors—expected to care for other children,
like my mother,
another child
only sixty-something years old,
turned out, in her turn, to forage and fend for herself.
We must stick together, we children, against the bullies
playing at corporations and governments and such.
So I am easy on myself
and gentle, so gentle.
I speak soft words to myself.
The words I say to me
always have a smile behind them;
a sprinkle of love and a little bit of awe.
I am careful to be gentle, and patient, and always

unfailingly kind
to me—
my precious, my priceless,
my first and forever love.

'contingencies'

She carries a condom in her purse
in case of rape.
When I saw it, I asked,
teasing,
expecting some joke or frisky comment—
"You never know when the craving will strike"
—something in that vein.
She answered in an off hand
distracted way,
as if she was telling me the time
or the way to the bathroom.
I stared at her, shocked.
When she noticed, she laughed
and began to explain about
walking with your head down,
not making eye contact,
being careful to respond to greetings,
giving away your number,
walking very quickly,
and weighing inflections of 'No.'
I asked her why she carried a condom,
not a knife.
She laughed and showed me a six-inch blade
tucked in a hidden pocket.
"I call this Plan A," she said,
a glint in her eye.
I asked her about decent people,
like, surely, society

and the Good Men in your life
will work together to protect you—
"Yes," she answered
dryly,
"who do you think gave me the rubber?
My father."

Henneh Kyereh Kwaku

Gaana & Other Poems

Playing God In Old Love Skin

tonight, we rehearse, again –
you're god
i'm the boy whose posters
dance in the wind
the boy whose black face
in the picture
on the posters makes him a crow
you, god – have given
the crow the wind
& here's the crow flying against
the gift & not gliding with it –
you say *take a bit more of white
& give me some black*
but your wind won't stop
& only the drowned hears
stay calm –
& obeys, not the drowning

The Magician

for Adedayo Agarau

he points to a spot on the enclosed
glass casing   he says, *direct the sound here, it'll break*
the blacksmith hammers where it is most important
to him, not to break
the metal   he tests the strength of his creation
he sharpens the metal so he gets a quick death
if he's impaled on it   one day
I was writing a poem once   about a dream where I am inside
the glass casing – where I was mastering the illusion
& the strength of my voice   I hammered it
at all the edges, I wanted it sharp enough to cut god's breath
I poured my voice out like ore & hit & hit & hit –
the glass never broke   in another dream
i'm the glass
& here's a man determined to break me

Gaana

"...he (soldier) [...] pointed the ri-
fle at the throat of Eric Ofotsu.
He shot without hesitation..."
– *Eyewitness, On the murdering of Eric Ofotsu*

I want to get a pet one day – a cat, maybe or a dog –
& name it after my country, so each poem I write for it,
is also for my country. I want a messy pet – a beautiful pet
a pet that's a metaphor for my country. That when I say
my pet tore my life apart today, I also mean – *my country tore my life apart.* When I say my pet is beautiful, I also am
saying – *my country is beautiful.* When it steals my fish,
I say what I say. When it brings me fish, I know there's
a bargain – something taken, something I won't know of.
When it breaks my heart, I know it is my country
& I cannot unlove it – when it kills me, I won't know.

Gabrial Awuah Mainoo

Seven Shapes Of God

…and a creviced sanctuary stood
above it was an altar without veil
above the altar was $7\times0=?$
A clergy stood on the conundrum
saying he was God.
I've known God in my holy leaves
He is not a colourless exocarp.
He may be of a sculpture, which blood is dribbled upon
like an "akuaba" in the shrine.
If He is fire
He must be pain.
If He is life
He must be death.
If anyone has seen God
it must be me, in my brother's dying face.
Once you chant what you have not seen
God must be a god Himself.
If He is black
He must be coal.
Should He be snow
He cannot be God.
But if snow could be God, then $0\times7=…$

Dream Boy

*and when you discover you gonna be in life,
set out to do as if God the almighty sent you at
this particular moment in history to do it.*
—*Martin Luther King J.R./*

In the wishing, comes
a remembered day
of starry reeds, lightning rivers
wearing a dream
you must make a cloud
of endless days
quiescent—
as the oblivious stream
incessantly darting
through the mire;
& drifting hope to where they've never been
to hatch a dream, lift it
from the haze,
coil a prayer around it, and name it sun
in the sailing, where
winds sweep pine boughs into the air
I have scrattled wounds for years
but I do not grieve, for that
the ending—because I know
a Black boy will crumble walls
rocking his body
against the night
Oh gold, oh sun
that is you—dream boy!

A Black Skin Breaks Away From Hell

I'll say it all…
the number of times I have walked the chimney
before I learnt moisture brings back the body
I have had seven thousand, seven hundred and seventy-seven scars
not on my body—
somewhere the vacuum,
in-between thoughts & guilt
anytime it rains, I am caught in a rim of tornadoes
as the shower ends, the sun spits,
caught in the furnace, I dance off-beat
mostly the madness comes at night
in the chaos of the silence
I yell, & my neighbours yell after me
I slip them into the madness
& they run with me
I run with the motive of jumping from the top floor
my skill is—
if I am drowning, I drown with all strength
sinking down the confusion
because my strength is weak
I come up the surface of my body
only to find the rope as a necklace/

Ruvimbo Chido Chikanda (RUBZI)

Hey Mr. Paradox

We began with the words, 'It's a pleasure to meet you!'
Tall and lanky yet an intriguing figure
A puzzling mindset that became the positive to my negative pole
Thy permanent dipole-dipole attraction keeping ye love atoll
A tall pillar of strength of toll-free experience of support
A toll of the bell as alarm of bewildered affection of some sort
A love so absurd
Completely unorthodox
It left me utterly baffled; his name became PARADOX.

Hello Mr. Paradox
Eccentricity that has knocked off my socks
My ultimate challenge to intellectually think outside the box
The bass guitar of a voice contradictory to the rubber ducky of a laugh
Guaranteed happiness and bliss ado, O how much I adore you.

Bonjour Monsieur Paradox
Now my penmanship is as proud as a peacocks'
Inscribing the accounts of my responsibility as your companion
Even through our childish irresponsible notions
Blooming petals of colourful emotions

Unforgettable moments
Our connection so potent.

Kwaziwai VaParadox
Our love is a sequel of Birdbox
Blind and finding its way down the riverside
Take my hand; let us wed by the nourished hillside
O please do make me your bride.
I'll take it ALL
The mystery here and the assurance in the other hand
Seventh heaven, I cannot even begin to comprehend

Hey Mr Paradox
I'm confused, but I understand…

Power Lenses

Focus! On yourself, of course
Pay attention, let all your being flow on, of course
your eyes have captured a tonne load of memories
visually analyse that reflection in the mirror
allow your gaze to bounce back
stare right into your soul
you'll be a fool to think that's all,
Now, be honest, what do you see?

Bipolar Bladder

I am a straightforward person,
with a bipolar bladder—you know how it is

When it's time to urinate,
you don't feel like it

When you can't urinate,
you really need to do it

How unfortunate!

Nothing is as cancerous as pee,
except for a cancerous cell itself

When the whole situation is still nonexistent,
you can solve it

But in due time,
it's way too late when you notice it

It's everyday life!

Christine Coates

Threnody for a Queen in Four Parts – an Opera

2. The Girl

Who is she – this one just like me,
another me. A mother.
A little mother, a mother before her time.
It is her birthday – time of Noël, birth of a god, before
the year dies. Is she an offering,
a sacrifice?
She brings forth a cub, cub
of the king. She is mother now,
the next mummy.
She leaves the cub in the care
of her old mother, the mother
clawing the Umsinsi tree.
She is searching, searching for her time.

She searches in the sands, but
her father's wind has come and blown away the traces.
Who are these creatures gliding
across the desert? Creatures of strength,
creatures of beauty.
Tall, purposeful sisters, they glide, they're wise.
I stand before them, bow.
One is baked clay, the other is bronze, the third stone.

4. The Collapsed Mother

"She's gone. Gone while I was sleeping." It's her boy, her
favour. He searches, searches.
"She shall not return," says the man in the pointed hat.
I left her here sleeping, peaceful on the couch.
"She shall not return."
He seeks her in every mountain shadow, seeks
beneath the rain, among the words of the bearded men,
where
her voice was an equal.
"She's gone, gone while I was sleeping."
The view from this end, her end –
her son is pulling through the sands, pulling on a rope,
an eagle cast in cement.
Did he have to kill the mother to marry
the father? He is rocking the kingdom's boat.
Was it all so oedipal?
She makes motley notes; I tried my best, but like Venus,
I am broken.
"Dress your family in corduroy and dreams," the women
wail.

Shah mat, shah mat. The game only ends
when the king is dead.
Now she's awake but not quite – all her children are
there,
her other son weeps quietly.
Will they tell her they love her? Do they?

Her daughter eyes the kingdom.

Kwaku Dade

To Aluah I

I slept early yesterday and woke up late.
I had no dream, but my mind tells me I am lying.
Four days since your stay at Tamale for work
and I am like a letter you penned for me,
only to burn when I unseal it.
I am home in Nsawam, but my mind tells me I am lying.
Here, days are long, nights, empty, piercing.
In my mind, you lurk about the house.
You splash in the bathtub, tap on the ceramic,
you are in the hall, in the kitchen, in the hallways.
But the walls whisper to me that I am lying.
I step into these your motions,
and I find only a brush of cold under my skin.
In our backyard, your hand touches mine, pegging
clothes on the drying lines,
and longings inside you transfer into me.
But the passing breeze screams into my face that you are not here.
In the sky, asperatus clouds form you,
naked, in a bed of bubbles.
You stare back at me with famished eyes
with a hint of detestation.
And sunlight pours through it all.
And it rains.
I remember us sleeping on our Tamale bed.
Our son sleeps between us, and when the void of dreams takes him,
I climb over to you;
I brush my cheeks against the silk of your stomach,

and our souls will dance
the dance of water and joy and release.
Our bed in Nsawam is haunted by old touches,
old motions, old laughter, old tears of ecstasy.
It is a cold hug. It holds me these days as a fetus,
and a blanket will only scrape me sore, and
I must only think of you.

I sniff the clothes you left behind.
You smell like dead flowers when you are not around.
I smile at your pictures and let my heartbeat kiss them.
This warms the flesh between my bones and stirs dregs
of our soft moments and of unfinished feelings.
I should have no dream in my sleep tonight
as I have not had one for thirteen nights.
But our bed tells me I am lying.
Because a dreamless sleep holds a thousand dreams
too rich with revelations to be recalled.
Because you are my consciousness and deep sleep.
You are my cure.
I am curing myself of this.
I am flying to Tamale tonight.

To Aluah II

From the time you became mine and I yours,
nothing is too beautiful, and ugly things are misnomers.
Extremes are normal. The loves I knew were worlds
where the more I shrank, the more I was beloved.
Pomp of fleeting fragrances, rhetoric without roots,
differences of others were faults and proof they were better;
I was the more parched when I drank from their idiosyncrasies.
I was in company with one of such, in cheer, but
when I was cheerful with my words, she preached on humility; and
when she saw her entourage coming our way,
she imposed I hold her bag of worries, imagine.
You in my life was an impossibility,
the solitude and healing I needed—and
good things happen when I return to stillness—
all the chaos, cacophony, turn music, and
you remain the thoughts that fill up the rhythm of my glory.
Your touches educate my skin's palate, I was green and
hard, and now I ripe; known and unknown parts of myself unify.
One thing about saving a life, the person lives for you,
I live for us. Remember the times when I am shaken by the good
within good you do for me, and I remain silent,
worry not, I mean every word I have not said.

We have simultaneous selves, I feel them; we read of each other's essences,
some on this Earth and the rest on other Earths.
I hear them in the heart of their hearts, grateful
to us that we aligned and by it recovers our time lost,
that all of us be liberated. Yours is where my strength stays,
that any entitled person is as good as a stone to me, and
when they come close to my soul, I throw them out the walls, and
from this is my compassion to myself. Our lives are but a prologue
of the lives of our children; we shall burn well for their spirit and
gifts to stay in enlightenment. Our deeds blur
into either salvation or voids. This dawn, I dreamed
I bathed buckets of water I did not fetch.
I splashed the last bucket into the air, and
I saw you reflected in every drop, and
they joined, floated up, became a cloud, froze, and
broke into blackness. You rub your palms into my palms and
wake me into your softness. My wings blow
out of my cocoon. All I desire is rain.

Building Beauty

I am the barrel of the gun that kills me,
and the bullets are a baby smiling at me.
My toddler's hand on my naked back in the morning to wake me up,
birds swarming the sky by indigo songs,
the colours and noise of the forest,
a whirlpool nebula breathing in and out binaural beats,
the green in a field stretching acres only to touch the silver of a lake,
obsessive compulsive happiness in peak bloom,
and my love's rangoli of kisses on my beaten body.
All these beauties, wearing what is home to my soul,
draw away from afar the will of the afternoon of my life
and invites me to embrace all that is and to rest.
Only that is not enough for me.
A preacher in the market square curses gossips
with his raised Bible. On the bus coming home, the passengers
mock at a man the radio said was arrested for stealing
seven bunches of plantain because his girlfriend asked
for a makeup set. But who knows what stole the gossips' time
for them to gossip? And who knows if the plantain thief
had great-grandparents whose wealth were squashed
by a bitter government, and he had to do anything necessary
to keep the family dignity intrinsic in him?
When we know everybody's full story,

we will know that nobody is a villain.
Annoyances of life, pleasures that the loins strive to equal,
no honey drunk without mixing with tears,
and attractions that make dwelling in moderation
as if kissing my own nipples test the soul's maturity;
our progresses in spite of it all add to the world's unfolding.
Only liars add nothing to the world.
Not accepting life as it is but diving headfirst
into my shadow and mine the mystery of myself,
with it floods of pain and devastations, and at the mecca of it
to ring-fence time for stillness to wake into a balance
of thoughts and being, and spiral through the paths
of my becoming as a murmuration of soul instincts;
and sometimes, my past intersects with my present, and I say,
"This all makes sense now. The gains of today are because of the failures of yesterday,"
and the revelation forms into a chisel by my Will
to hack at my attitude until it is only soul and my intuition,
and at this to give of all that I am into a higher turn,
and that, too, is beauty, which
only women know too well how to handle.

Jeremy T. Karn

Portrait of a Liberian's Boy & Other Poems

Portrait Of A Liberian's Boy

about an anonymous boy
how do you hold another boy's blood in your body?
it will only dissolve
into nothing.
you have had another boy
deep inside you;
this made your body a tunnel
pushing things within,
inch by inch until you grew flowers in your pores

you've been walked too much into,
breaking your body
into a woman

this explains it,
the softness that haunts your body,
the song that sits in your silence

I remember the green ceiling light,
bleaching your half-naked body through the dark keyhole
your shirt rolled above your belly like a map;
it peeled out the hardness on your tongue
& made you a small god

2020, tonight your body burns with memories; it itches for his smell
mother thinks you've replaced the devil
by calling another boy's name in your sleep

Sickle Cell Anaemia

for A. Sheriff II

from birth, you have been trained by your father on how
to die
now you're bored of breathing
it makes you too perfect at dying
I have seen your fresh footprints over graves

it's no secret you love the sea,
the warmness of your mother's hands
on your bones, cracked
like the living room's wall

she, too, is praying for your death

you want to die your own death
from your own sickness
ingest songs that'll plant seeds in your body for a rebirth

but how long will you keep lying in bed,
practicing how to turn your bed into a coffin?

some day, you will weigh the pain that carves
the smell of death in your breath

some day, you will pinch yourself into nothing,
begging your body to fall into an open grave

The Making Of Grief

I

out of cries, I have made songs
I sometimes
hum in my sleep, deep under my skin

I shovel out memories out of my body
plant silence in it
I have watched my silence grow into nothing;
my mother says it can move a mountain

II

there are things sadder than death,
like smoke that gains its existence
from a body on fire

the way cigarettes burn in Monrovia
reminds me of you – dead & burning in the brown soil

it stripped your body into ashes,
but a body on fire is the origin of grief

the fumes from your burnt body,
I have lived with the scent long enough

Phodiso Modirwa

Another Dirge To Fill The Space Left Behind

I wish I had known you would not return from the war/work
You with your big, beautiful heart
Opening up to us like ripe pomegranate
Offering us it's bursting sweetness; from inside, it's a brown
cover, like your skin

I did not know then that that summer was our last
But I would have still loved you even if I knew forever wasn't ours
Knew you weren't mine to epistle into these poems decades later
My words, hesitant children stooping at the foot of their grandfather's grave
Their questions, a third generation of prayers without aim/amens

Into the emptiness that stayed behind to haunt me
You said
I will be back
instead of
Goodbye
Cast a spell on me I cannot undo any other way
But to sing endless eulogies to lure you back to here

Sometimes I fear you will tire of all these songs

With their melody so old and spent

But even if I had known you would not return
from the war inside your body, a cancer I cannot pronounce,
I would have loved to hear you say it
Say that you're tired and leaving
Instead, you said you were fine
Then took the early morning bus forever into the unknown

Talking To My Mother About My Job (After Henneh Kyereh Kwaku)

I want to get a plant one day—a money plant or cactus perhaps—and name it after my job, so each
poem I write for it is also for my job. I want a detached plant, a touchy plant, one that latches onto me as it grows, and one that can go weeks without the kiss of my watering can's mouth. When I say my plant is
taking over my life, I mean my job is taking over my life. When I say my plant is refreshing to have, I also
mean my job is useful to keep. When it yellows around the edges, I say what I say of deprivation. When it remembers its green [of money or life]—I know there is a bargain—something taken, something I
won't know of. When it breaks my heart, I know it is my job, and I cannot leave it. When it kills me, I
won't know.

Cento: Investigating Lonely

I want my own pain to be intimate (Jones)
I won't know to daughter till its done (Wheeler)
Maybe I am unloved because I want to trade in the currency of ghosts (Carino)
But I wanted to see how many languages love could be dished in (Prempeh)
What do we call the girl who looks away from herself—a spook? (Maluluke)
All night I be trying to make sense of my name, to love whatever is left (Guest)
I remember how long it took to own this bulb of joy (Queeney)
Memory, now that's a thing a girl can get behind (Williams)
Though I wish I could be alive in several ways more than this one (Ndwuko)
But aren't we all alone in the end? (Limon)

Lesley Wheeler
Ina Carino
N K A Prempeh
Vuyelwa Maluleke
Paul Guest
Maggie Queeney
Adele Elise Williams

Joseph omoh Ndukwo
Ada Limon

Taofeek Ayeyemi

Three Haibun
Twist Of Fate

You sit on a stool at the veranda of the house where you are a squatter, measuring the length of freedom and independence with your imaginary ruler; you see them stretching like the extreme of a desert. You weigh the aura of inconvenience and discomfort that bask in the air around you; it feels like it overwhelms the earth so much that it sinks into the seven oceans. You imagine how you have to take things calm lest you open your cup of salt and find maggots. This is not what you wanted, but life is an enigma. Yet, hope ticks with each beat your heart makes, daily, like the hands of a temple clock. You want to untake the ridicule staining your skin and undo every disregard, but your bank account balance keeps disarming you. And when you stare well, you realise no one is fighting you. No one dare confronts you with ridicule, but fate.

flooded fields . . .
a rodent paddles
a maize stem

Per Diem

Lying on a sofa, occasionally sniffing your arm for the stench of a poorly-dried, long-spilled water, you think of how you stretch your hand daily to receive your pay, like Al-majiri. You shake your head, again and again. And the words of the three-year-old boy that recently went viral on the internet slips into your mind: "I am smart. I am blessed. I can do anything." You rise, like the head of a king cobra, and say the same to yourself, your hand on your chest.

migration—
the treetop leaves shaken
by eagles' flight

Colour By Colour, Re-painting My Dreams

Before me is a candelabra of seven branches—in each branch is a lit candle of its own colour: red, black, brown, yellow, blue, green, white. And as if they're not acknowledged, I raise my head to the moon, capture its stellar rays inside my mouth, imagine it slipping down my throat, and I become a body of light, a luminous thread weaving beads of glee into the night. I capture the lit candles in my mind; their flames burn the veil against the eyes of the bird of my soul—and it flaps its wings, trembles with the flicker of the candle, and rises with the smoke of the incense. My body is here, but my soul has transited to the terrestrial sphere through the web of my spirit—like a thread connecting a nylon kite and the player. In the confine of my vision (a string of cryptic dreams inside a dream), I see my soul—now humanoid—cloister out into an orchard, pick leaves and measure their weight, feel their textures on its cheek, sniff their fine and harsh scents, picks stones of shapes, sizes, and colours, and reach the understanding of fate and faith. Walking in silence, from silence into a deeper silence, and carrying tranquility on its tongue and visage, it enters a cubicle for a lustral bath, after which it slides down the luminous thread of my spirit, like a spider, back into my body. I half-open my eyes; my mouth carries the taste of salt, the candles have burnt beyond half, their lights flickering.

autumn meditation—
the cat on the door mat takes
the shape of yoga

Bryan Obinna Joseph Okwesili

Preacher Man Knows My Name

The first thing that is taken away
from LGBT people is our spirituality
-Billy Porter

Sunday hymns remind me of cassocks swooshing in
the wind, marked white with holiness.
I have always loved this picture, a boy
learning to say, who made you? God made me.
After a long while, he plucks it from
his mouth, wondering why it is something
he cannot swallow. Preacher man knows my name.
He holds it in his palms and puts it beside the
things he says must burn to be saved.
I have been told I need to be saved, many a time, that
my prayers only stop halfway to heaven and begin
a descent; a walk of shame home to me.
Beside these candles, I have cried myself into a
penance, seeking the face of God in the beads of
rosaries strung around my neck like a leash,
wanting to be led to the pulpit, to be led into the
light, like the preacher man says.
But I have seen Billy Porter wear a gown
into a camera, and I do not believe an art from God
could be impure, could need saving.
I have seen his smile strike light

into a photo before owning it. It is a thing about believing
your God takes your face, and you, in the moment of living,
let him shine through.

Chi is how we say it in Igbo—one's personal god—
and I have seen mine sweep her hair into a bun,
before reaching out to hug me into a happy thing.
One must feel the river try to become him, before one
can sing of drowning. I am afloat. I can see the sun
above me, the wind behind my ears, gentle.

My chi rows me, by and by, past the hymns of
a catholic church. The bells sway their heads into a dong.
I can see cassocks swooshing in the distance.

My Prayers Do Not Promise Me Heaven

If you do not condemn me too, pray for me
tonight, as I fold this wreath into a halo.
My prayers do not promise me heaven.
It is like saying sinners are saints clothed in sin.
Tell God a man wielding a gavel stole his name.
Say it before an 'Amen,' then speak nothing of how
I died trying to live.

Try dying before living.
Be dust and be dust again.
Die, Homo! An abrupt condemnation.
How do you punctuate hate?

Gaze upon my face as I shut my eyes,
embracing this darkness. Pray!
After this life is another life, like an attachment
to a letter, authored by a stranger with
a familiar face.
I am living but without light,
and pain.

He Hatched Into A Howl

I have called God twice.

When I leapt into the street as a child,
I was reminded to strap my hips with stiffness.
That swaying was what boys did before they began
to touch other boys.
At seven, I lost my strap to a choking night.
This was before I was called a seedling of Sodom,
before I was spooned disgust from loud mouths,
before welts glowed green, then red, on my skin.
With each stroke of pain, I could no longer house
God in my throat. He hatched into a howl.

When I strayed into a boy's heart and
bumped into things I liked, he promised me everything.
Take. Take it all, he said, that it was
the thing about love to have one thing
and lose everything.
I have you, he said.
And he lost himself to an early lump in his kidney.
In the darkness of my room, I rolled God
in my voice and raised it to heaven.
I did not want light.
I wanted my lover, who promised me company in the dark.

And I have been alone for far too long;
learning to love this darkness, this stillness.

Who lied of singing free birds?
I am chained to my thoughts, but I can sing.
A dirge is a song, too; a sorrowful pleasantness
for this lingering fate.

Because God is the only intruder without fault,
I have learnt to say welcome before I begin to cry.

Amirah Al Wassif

Human Tragedy

The holes that carved upon my forehead
Reveal how old I am.
My children had eaten their self
From a very young age.
I'm the mother
Who peels the hours?
With the patience's knife.
Watching their severed heads
Sparkling from upstairs
Like stars.
I am the mother, I shout,
Trying to call them by the name.
My children are so many,
Some on the trees,
Some behind the clouds,
Some riding horses in the sky,
Some washing their bodies
In my veins.
Some rubbing their noses
In the heart of your fresh towels.
Although, they have died,
For long centuries,
There are no signs of
Their death.
No gravestones for them.
I'm the only one
Who grieves over them?
I'm here, standing in pride.

Don't come for me.
I'm the mother, I shout,
The darkness cutting my throat.
I'm the detailed tale.
My children aren't your bruises;
They are the rhythm of
Your breath.
Although, they all died,
This isn't the end of the world.
We must have fun;
Sometimes you have to turn
Your lights off
For the sake of
Bathing in the moonlight.

Diaries From Jail

Between my teeth, there is a gap—
That kind could disturb a whole content.
My history began the very moment I escaped away from the herd.
When the leaves of our trees turned from green to red.
When our leader's head became our new sun.
The children circled around me, pushing me violently with such great force.
They have believed the rumours that said I belong to the dangerous genre who
dare to dream.
I have been trapped by the religious gang.
I screamed at my people's faces.
They planned to tuck me in the obedience pocket.
I had no one on my side, so I cupped my hands and knelt down to ask their mercy.
Stop dreaming! they cried out.
I yelled in a miserable tone; my heart sank in fear.
They built an ironic box for me, but I lived like a bird that sees itself in a larger
place, although its body is still caged.

Hallucinations

I had a dream of cows leading some people
Who were humming an old-fashioned poem.
The sound of the flute was coming out from the teeth of an ancient oak tree.
In that dream also, there was a moon and a half, falling into my mother's lap.
She was stitching a great piece of the sky upon the little heads of three terrified
cats.
I had a dream of being a gorilla.
The dirt was caked perfectly with my fingers.
I was another version of myself
Peeping into another world
Bathing in another water.
My body had billions of rooms
Empty ones without guests.
I was closed to be a river
But the temptation to be something bigger
Made me kneel
Swerving like a verse
Hovers like an angel's napkin.
Shivers like a love song
In a poet's chest.

Prince Rayanne Chidzvondo

The Stink

Today, there's no water from the damn taps again
Without water, we can't even flush down the damn system
So it stinks, for years on end, with fattening worms wriggling their tiny brains full of shit

Allegedly

Men in my family soaked themselves in bleach to clean the last remains of affection
They scrubbed the reek of compassion, scrubbed and scrubbed until they could scrub no more
They completely removed their skins and hung them up as displays off their inherited manhood
They walk as broken skeletons, keeping enough secrets to make them holy
They cut off their tongues to remain indifferent, unmoved, something uncaring
They signal the siren of their egos in every room they enter
breaking everything in which they can not fill...
My body did not dip in bleach
My body did not clean out the affection
My body did not scrub itself clean of the reek of compassion
I did not remove my skin to hang it on things not natural to it
I feel and express with every fibre of my being

Every room of me is a verse and a metaphor, each feeling a pole in the skin I embraced
I am still trying to praise my own name on days I can remember it
Yet still, I, too, cut off my tongue when they called me a man
Allegedly, I said to myself, just like stories about them, allegedly, of cause

Days Of July

(Written during the Covid Pandemic)

breaking news
from the corner of a dimly lit
restaurant
forecast says we'll be awaiting
clear skies
you continue to wear your mask and
wash your hands

I am dust
learning to navigate through
the intricacies of our lives
we have lost all conversation
choosing only the things
that make us less uncomfortable

it seems my predictions haven't
gone as planned
awaiting sunlight and tranquillity
I have been fooled by the long

downpours of your tears
in the evening
the violet flares on the bus rides home
I can never seem to get what I want
the system makes us all so needy

headlines and expensive newspapers
you curse about it under your breath
prices are going up every day
tension is building
and I find myself uneasy with all this warfare
winters have never been kind
we are nowhere and everywhere
of course, I feel too much
I am a universe of exploding stars

I thought I would feel something
significantly greater than the last month
yet here I stand, feeling indifferent
I can not say this is how I wanted things to go
with all the unpredictability and confusion
we are both yearning for the same ending
in the meantime
we wash our hands and wear our masks

the breaking news that you missed is
I don't remember your smile

Londeka Mduli

The Sky Has Robbers

We cracked the sky open and found window frames full of
Robbers lying in between the stars, the dust settling
Like a pair of drunk lovers on a Friday night.
The sun and its coffee whispered, "There is no theft here"
But there are piles of brown bodies that only wish to look like us.

Pigeon Houses

When you return home, find me a cilantro pigeon
Bring back the cotton mouth hair and watch me hang
The moon with your plots,
Ask me, why butterflies without wings are just
Caterpillars aspiring to be the birds that eat them.

Immigration

They leave the war before the water comes,
they stood still with their sticks in silence,
and the tide washed away empty mouths,
Ghosts hung over waves, hoping to return home,
but it is night-time, and there are no more bones left to sing to,
and I am no coyote to drag the leaves out of the water.

Richard Mbuthia

Wistful Wisps

Lying here, dejected,
banging my head on the wall behind me,
my pillow all soggy with tears from tired eyes,
sorry notes rising from the bleeding well
in the dark recesses of my being,
and you come, all styled up
with words rehearsed, rehashed:
to cool my boiling mind;
to pull my tattered soul,
and you think it'll work with me this time...

You want to fish me out of despondency
with quotes from men of old
with verses from the Bible
with words from the Koran
with epithets scrawled on ashen walls -
and you think it'll work with me this time...

My heart is immune to fireless rumblings -
You know: a cold hearth cooks no meal!
I need more than words
to lift me out of this miry bog...

Fish me not with eyes of steel
that cut to the marrow;
Fish me not with paper cords
that can't stand their own weight.

Extend your soft hand -
reach out and lift my frail self;
resuscitate me with love divine,
As I lie supine:
Looking into your eyes...
locking my heart to yours!

Edible Bubbles

Munching through the edible stillness of time –
my soul afire,
my heart astir,
with expectations of a bloated mind
As I sit at the table of life's offerings,
I doodle the day's meal in colour.

The onions roll my way
Peeling off their layers –
...lairs of crusty feelings
Revealing succulent reds and whites
to embittered hot oil
that spatters and splatters on the kitchen floor!

With the dexterity of an African politician
stealing an election at sunrise –
I chop tomatoes;
I slash the cabbage;
I cut the meat,
gingerly balancing emotion with fortitude!

The meal of life is an elaborate affair:
The feisty peeling, cutting, chopping,
Add rhythm to the ancient pacemaker
That harbours poetry in rivers of red
In a cage of meshed cartilage and bone
As livid oil impatiently bubbles!

Crumbs Of Life

I am a slice less as a loaf of self…
Each dot of crumb, a life;
each facet's face, a turn;
A mirror—a voice with an edge.

Self-discovery bludgeons the conscience—
as the sore festers and runs,
The loaf, unconcernedly… obscenely…
lights a smoke, roasting deflated lungs.

The loaf—white, brown, starched, mouldy
All seasons of life in the trenches of reason;
fired volleys… ceasefires—the racket—
ricochet off the crumbs' firewalls!

I am a slice less as a loaf of self…
And in the fell clutch of circumstance
I neither see, hear nor feel
the pain of a beautiful loss!

Timothy Fab-Eme

Ecocide In The Wake Of Discovery And Dreams

Poppa rises, waves his hand and whistles like a rooster;
that's how he tells me to steer the canoe well.
Darkness has a way of magnifying lack—our oil lamp
isn't helping much now—it's the sort of night folk
say the moon refused to eat, leaving a sad sky;
the clouds clap, the river raves and poppa sighs heavily,
it will rain again tonight, he'd said in the morning,
and I believed him because his knees are rain sensors.
The rope of hope twirls in his hands until it
strains like a thunderbolt. I'm used to being a spate
of reveries—three, too old to be a child—thirteen,
too young to be in school—I've mastered the art
of mummifying dreams. He tugs the net—its weight limning
the delta the night Shell drilled oil rigs into her womb;
he gains two arms, six… nothing. What fish doesn't swim?
Poppa pulls again, and the cast net tears. He climbs
down sadly as cold cups his scrotum; he emerges as
a mad masquerade, his lips dancing to the harsh harmattan.
He reenters the canoe, dripping crude oil: fish bones, plastics,
crab shells, mangrove leaves are the fish in the fishnet.
What lives in the Niger Delta? What's alive here? What?

We're Sick Now And Earth's Healing Real Fast Spring

COVID-19 has shut us in, like a despot,
and all our love for oil and gas
and negative science has become naught as noise.
We're resting from NBC and VOA breaking news
about trade wars, petty politics and greedy folk.
We're sick now, and Earth's healing real fast;
a grand submit is on in the Sahara—
everyone's there except Human. Coyote sits still
on a dinner table with Wolf talking about
the unusual peace they've got. Zebra and Lion
mock Human for gathering things she doesn't need
to live, like nuclear arms and diamond rings.
Of all creatures, Tortoise says, Human's the most
pitiable. Reckon God's regret about the damn thing?
We're sick now, and Earth's healing real fast.

Echoing Loss As A Prelude To The Opera Of Bad Regimes

It hurts, you know, to call this hell home.
My cousin, with the hair of aloe vera leaves,
jogged out one morning to sweat away his frustrations
the way grandma squeezes out oil from palm fruits.
He was disappeared like flotsam; the police said Bobby
has the eyes of thieves, lips of gays, and a murderer-smile.
Three days later, the newspapers and TVs headlined him
a drug dealer, armed robber, rapist, cultist, gangster, fraudster,
and other sandy names that end with a pause;
I cocked my mouth's speargun and shot cusses everywhere.
In other words, Bob wasn't tried—in other words,
they didn't give us his body—in other words,
we couldn't dress his wounds and name him properly;
we only cried like a crashing engine, picked his
favourite shirt and scribbled an epitaph with our teardrops.

Nebeolisa Okwudili

The Making Of Widows

I would often remember this event
with slight changes, a necessary thing
to be reckoned with, our bungalow
appearing smaller each time I came home,
my mother on the phone speaking with
one of our cousins living in Warri
where she had lived with her elder sister.
Or maybe it was my mother's retelling
of her own family, detached from
the real family after her father died,
and his property was split among the boys
as if the remaining did not belong.
And then her elder sister's husband died,
and her brother-in-laws sauntered in—
she said it was raining the whole week
they came, the rain beating against the zinc roof
so that the men had to raise their voices
and the women, arms folded, listened.
My mother said she remembered those days
even up to the glint of sunlight
distilling the louvers anytime
it didn't rain, the long conversations
that never tapered into laughter,
her sister folding and unfolding her arms
as her in-laws portioned the things to themselves.

Beggars

After the words of a friend

"One way or the other, you guys have made us
beggars in every sense of the word:
begging for our visibility,
then begging for our rights, to walk the streets
and not to be stoned in front of the children,
begging not to be preached against in the church,
begging not to be heroes, begging to be
normal citizens, begging to marry,
begging to have children, begging to walk
into a store and not to be turned back
before we had even purchased our wares,
begging not to be shot in the bars, begging
not to be killed in our sleep, or burned,
or worse still, doused in acid, begging
to hold hands in the streets, begging to hold
meetings in public buildings, begging
to drink in the open, begging to be
alive, begging to see the doctor.
Last night, my friend couldn't tell the doctor
why he had a haemorrhoid, that two men
the previous night had spiked his drink
and taken him to their apartment.
Please don't call it an us-to-us crime.
My friend is begging to be seen, he can't
explain to the doctor why he needs
his blood tested, aside from the tablets

and suppositories that were prescribed.
My friend is not wayward. In a sane clime,
he should report this to the police, but the men
he should be reporting to will arrest him first
after he must have tabled his case.
Once again, my friend is a beggar.
Sometimes, I wake up and wonder if
wearing pink is not crossing the line,
if the shirt I want to put on with the trouser
will appear like the combination
a woman would love to be putting on,
if a woman is not seeing me
in herself, but then I could be all the things
you want and more, but not every day.
Like me, my friend is tired of being brave
or being a beggar, of having to ask.
After a long time, even soldiers
desire to be back from the war."

A Myth In Two Parts

I

At one time, we were considered wizards.
At another time, we were prophets.
There had to be something mystic about us
since the doctors couldn't remedy us
of the depravity, since the spirits
hovering inside us couldn't be chased,
since punishing us did not make us change.
I heard we were once custodians,
but of other spirits, it is not clear
what type of spirits it must have been,
if their motives were clean or obscene.
At that time, it was considered witchcraft,
as craft but not as diabolical.
That we didn't find love in the other sex
made us mystical. Possessed by a female,
most likely a witch, we sought for love
in the same sex of our bodies, if body
were but a containing vessel,
if sex were merely a product of the mind
independent of the body, if sex
was the thing that made a man desire
to be probed by another man in the night.

II

Some myths had it that these spirits

occupied bodies in the night through dreams
that a woman's body could wake up
one morning and start feeling like a man,
that the main portal was through wet dreams.
There had to be some bodily fluids exchanged
as a form of transcendental transaction
in the spirit realm, which is why a man wakes up
only to notice that his milk had spilled
from his body, and in some lore, the exchange
could not be revoked in the same way
that marriage is till death do the parties part.
A man occupies a woman's body
and owns her forever—but a man,
sometimes, is surprisingly owned by a man
who is not interested in looking at women.
This part of the ownership was not explained.
The most confounding part of the myth
was that the spirit, on its own, bored
of existing in an inactive body,
could up and leave or return with more
and that was their explanation for those ones
who, this month, lived with a man and the next,
sought for love in the arms of women.

Leroy Mtulisi Ndlovu

The Minister Of (Good) Will

In the news a lot,
Some say he's a twit.
'Just a load of rot!'
That's what they call it.

'We'll do this and that,'
he says, wiping his brow,
'We'll fix it all up. Stat!
No need to panic now!'

'I will call this Minister,
And ask for this favour.
Together we'll administer
solutions you'll favour.'

His employers are starving.
They have been for years.
He cares not a farthing;
He's been eating their tears.

His portfolio of promises
Gets bigger and bigger.
Now the older crowd's (bellies) miss
Being called niggers.

A Shopping Expedition During Lockdown

Grinning as if he were the rabbit,
Singing over the hare's bones,
The Assistant Inspector leads four
Past the queueing smartphones.
His associates, Male Constable,
Constables Big Booty and Thigh Gap,
Stand by the door, counting tattered notes.
And as Alpha Indie passes, each one dips their cap.
A Sargent materialises, and the male constable
Gives him what looks like fifty bonds.
Out here, in three queues in the sun,
The rest of us burn like over-baked scones.
Two queues for Chibataura to the left and right
And another for groceries, airtime & 'tron.'
All three are controlled by the boys and girls in blue
With help from their highly-trained and well-fed Alsatians.
Assistant Inspector returns with more notes in hand
And the observer's pen runs with a little less patience.

A Looter Contiua

The girl stood in the aisle
Watching the adults awhile.
She stored in her mind's vault
The memory of stolen salt
And sugar beans held tight.
Parents went from love so tender
To each other's main contender.
So here Sibonginkosi stood,
Another starving neighbourhood
Stat of the domestic fight.
Her mother didn't raise a fool:
She picked up books for school
And a bar of soap for cleanliness.
The store was such a screaming mess
As S'bonginkosi ran away.
Now she holds her pen so tight,
Blocking out her parents' fight,
and praying soldiers stay away.

Pusetso Lame

Botswana

Her back carries us like her dearest children
She walks us down the Okavango waters to the sand dunes in
Kalahari
Our tongues cannot stop praising her amazing nature
53-year-old beauty that still glows
My pride in the national anthem
Fatshe leno la rona (This is our country)

Thoughts

Just like a midnight mood
I would love to hug the shadows of all those crying out
in
misery
Like a slow jam song
I would like to take one step at a time out of those hurtful
moments
For just like the falling snow
I'd love to make the woman, with a bruised face from the
beatings she got last night, smile
Just like a hymn
I would love to comfort you with my lyrics
Soothing your heart when all you can think of is extinction
When all you can see is a worthless being
Trying to resurrect from a grave that keeps digging itself
deeper and deeper
Like rain droplets
I'd slowly but surely wipe away all the pains from yesterday's
rejections
When all the doors before you have been closed even
before
your existence
For once, I'd love to be a pillow you shed your tears on
So that when the sun rises,

I would carry your fears in a piece of cloth and let them dry in
the sun
I'd love to be me as I deal with the inner man

Dear Death

Hey, it is me again
I know you are just a phone call away
But I wanted to ask you about something

You remember the day I wore a mini skirt to a priest's
funeral
One nun said you are not far from reaching me, too
Apparently, she thinks I have sinned against her God

Now, I want you to know something
I am only in my early twenties
I haven't been to Paris yet
I know my plea sounds too absurd, but it's true
I think I want to see how the world looks like before I
travel
with you

I've seen you snatching souls that still had more to offer
Than just expired oxygen and crushed bones
I have heard widows shouting out at midnight, cursing
the day
you knocked at their doors
I've watched my mother starving herself to the core on
most
days
Now, before the nun's words come to pass,
Remember my dream

It's not about Paris, but the modesty of falling in love with all
the places
It's maybe about the plea to let my toes feel the grounds my
ancestors never walked on
So, before coming here, knocking like a lost angel
Kindly be reminded of my plea

Nsah Mala

Forbidden

Hello, my reader!
Drop me not down
Once you've begun to drown
Your reading tentacles into me, reader.
These verses you read
Are my skeleton wrought with a reed,
A hollow reed that stains
The world with words and strains
To anchor wisdom to hearts,
Like Cupid anchoring love to hearts.
Divorce me not and turn
Not to liquor bottles to dissolve
Reason; rather resolve
With me to grasp the Crown in turn
When silent chances sail slowly
And at lightning speed but surely
Into our impatient dragnets
While we browse internets
Of prayers and chant them upwards
And espouse the Lamb to leap forwards.
(Mbankolo, 30 November 2012)

Sometimes I Wonder

*(From personal experience and
that of Ndikechu Greg.)*

Sometimes I wonder whether
the Soa-Ngoa rectors
know this:
that in computer central units,
students' marks
are swapped
for coins, for wads, for sex and for tribes;
that students' results
walk away
'never to return'
like Head's Elizabeth;
that some offices
on campus are brothels...
Sometimes I wonder whether
wind can't
inform ministers of this:
that innocent files
have aged to death point
in callous drawers
in some ministerial offices
because their owners
either
did not dissect wallets
or
were accidentally born

to babble
the Queen's Tongue
or turned down fondling invitations...
Sometimes I wonder whether
the powers that be
know this:
that some of these less-brains
who flood our professional schools,
divorced from merit,
and got married to
money migration
before punishing these tired desks;
that names were murdered
from among final lists
on their way
to billboards...
Sometimes I wonder whether
the mute statues in church
can't inform priests of this:
that these front-seat black suits
and white gowns
who change cars like
a chameleon changes colours
raise and swing
their hands too
in Lucifer's assemblies;
that God frowns at priests
who create artificial scarcity
of Holy Water,
making it a luxury
reserved only for generous thieves
and greedy neighbours
who dance up for second and third offertory baskets.
(Mbankolo, 16 August 2012)

Cloudy Day

(In memory of a terrible day in my life, November 15, 2012)

1.
The horizons open wide eyes
To peep on Earth.
Hunger's sons and daughters
Hit hard on my stomach's doors.
Then orphaned fried egg
And yellowish naked
Cassava powder (garri),
Baptized in hot Jordan,
Bid them welcome.

2.
Another clouded-sunny day is born.
To Nlongkak Governor's Office
I leap lousily and doubtfully,
With borrowed smiles
On my face sprayed
To conceal distrust.

3.
Rivers of cloudy file-chasers
Flood and flood the place,
Firing Ewondo verbal squads
Into my rioting mind and ears,
Reminding me to trust none

In this thorny battlefield,
Where every smile
Sheds layers of distrust
And dishonesty.

20
And fraud
And famine
And decay
And disgust.

4.
Yet Tanyitiku Egbe implants
Her roots of confidence
Into these sandy soils
And disagrees to agree
With me that the Kamerun desert
Is void of trust oases
And full of oceans of deceit.

5.
After aeons of hopeless waiting,
The clouded medical booklets
Cruise into our fatigued palms.
These medical booklets,
These medical booklets,
Struggling under
Conspicuous and suspicious
Signatures and stamps
From ghost-renowned medics
To declare our aptitude
To serve the State.

6.

Medical booklets?
Yes, medial booklets,
But never ask
And put to task.

21
The stethoscopes
And microscopes
That examined us
Because they all died
In the next
Clinical operation...

7.
My heart and mind clad in Thomas suits,
I brave hot and menacing solar spears.
Then I vamoose into ENS Yaoundé's
Département de Français of fears,
Knock and knock and knock like an Angel,
But no answers emerge from within.
Then unawares I take her
Like Palestinians to Israelis did on Yom Kimpur.
Her lips and teeth are at work,
Busily burying a loaf of bread.
"Monsieur Fouda vient de sortir,"
Answers my gentle request
For my own transcript
Whose application letter
Has for three weeks
Been dancing one tune here:
"Monsieur Fouda n'est pas là."

8.
Like a serpent that has swallowed a rat,

I drag along my heavy self to Ngoa-Ekelle
For another transcript of mine.
Indeed, even frustration is graded!

9.
Not only do I knock on Scolarité door
As if on a mortuary door,
but there my eyes are cursed to see
An adult woman wailing like a waterfall
In this deaf and dumb office,
After all her efforts to get a BA testimonial
Have been shattered and scattered by
Franco-frustration and flung
Down the cliffs of surrender
Where death watches
All victims through
Suicidal lenses...

10.
"Enough is enough,"
I resolve in me,
Deep, deep down in me
And haste homewards,
Ready to break the barracks
Of Kamerun like Takwi
When time and God
Join my cleansing team.
(Mbankolo, 16 November 2012)

Isaac Kwaliba

The Art Of Self De-struction

To prop
Diatribe with words of unfeel, you are too tired to grieve.
The end of today is not the anticipation it should be
Of tomorrow.
Look
A gift from war decades dead, don't touch me,
I'm a dead bee.
For DRC, for Sudan and Nigeria,
I'm too tired to live.

I lumber in marshes of blood feuds
The squelch of hooves a marching cant.
To dance in whorls, freed in the whirlpool of thought,
To heckle in the laughter of night and
Deride our childhood,
About how you and I are the only ones that know Tanzania.
How many wars did you spark?
How you fell into pits of violence, you could light the world.
Now we bandy soft words and nudge
With gentle banter.
I clamber onto trains of thought
and the people I hold hands spit,

Maybe this gift is a way to celebrate you,
And maybe I'm restless because I write of everywhere but home.

To decor
Beds with dreamcatchers, they come to dance
And find mushrooms on their graves.
I'm too tired to weed
The beards of whimsical consciences.

Deaf-blind

she lectures about haptic signs, and I think of you born
in the mid-morning how you hold my hand between
yours
and rub my twitchy fingers into a daze and speak empty
onto the seasonal rivers
kiss the desert twitch your nose sneeze into my armpit
now you teach me language in mother tongue

swahili music is the braille on your thighs dipped in the
contemplation of dates

I'm at a wedding in the month of fast waiting upon night
touch does not lie let your tongue only kiss
and not know the taste of half truths
sweet not to see nor to hear the paintings and readings of
love the corruption of passion

& I don't know if I love as the normal do, but you do as
no one else has
you sit with me on a balcony of make belief where we
conjure the spellings of green stars
and my eyes are moons you shine onto
I ask you to tell me about life and you say you are the
strongest woman in the world
you are.

I wave, like I'm made of flags and wish I was a mast content and holding, cusped

in the fury of a lover, could I hold wind in my belly
I choke, I'm no man: I'm no god, whose words are these?
be calm these demons the fog of writer's block wails in
the trees on my head
and lifts, unwilling in my nazarene.
I'm flying one foot after the other and the world grows
no walls
I could bump into, break my fall.

It Is What It Is

closer to earth, closer to betrayal
they strip for unripe moons we tell them to
slow and in deliberate uncertainty like a red indian in the fall of
mystic intoxication
like rastafari in the smoke of dezarie's voice
the veins on my face are like bony, lonely fingers or
throbbing rootlets. I jig, miss, do a half step, jerk
before I speak in tongues and spurt blood.

whose voice, whose heart is this?
like a son of the soil (hello templer!) at a tiriki shrine, so many likes
in this african bush I am unfurling me in the voice that declares
we are but dust: animated dirt…

Nehemiah Omukhonya

Shall We Live!

They say the apple doesn't fall far from the tree
But sometimes the tree holds onto the apple
So it doesn't fall
For the apple is safer in the tree than on the ground
And the topography may have it rolling;
Wandering into dangerous territory

After the fall, the lucky ones live under the tree
But the majority get devoured
Or move from vendor to vendor
Confined in bags with limited aeration
At the mercies of heartless beasts
With price tags as their identity

See, we may never feel protected anymore
It's certain we will never be young again
Perhaps we are older than our brains can really decipher
But we can always rekindle the feelings
Feelings that had us wear the most genuine smiles
We shall live!

Shame

I saw the moon crawl the sky
While I was busy running the earth
Still, my speed couldn't match the moon's

Maybe the race was even
Until dark clouds clothed the moon
Inviting vicious rains to this battle
That bred chaos and confusion
So I fled in search of order

I was happy to shelter under the sun
For the rains were too selfish to consider my pleas
I feared getting wet, but got burnt instead

The sky always frowned when I was in the picture
The stars were too afraid to come to my rescue
Still, I blamed me for trying to find safety
Because I was a disgrace, a sellout
For soldiers don't resign to fate, they fight!

Ann Pendo

No

Will, I ever forgive myself
For the days
I could have said no
I should have said no
But I half-heartedly said yes
I should have said no
Now I wallow,
In regrets
With flashes of how I dug my own hole
I said Yes
When I
I could have said No
I should have said No

A Night

Mother, I am back
With my whims
On my feelings
There's a boy
Need I say a man
He sees me
He sees me not
Mother my heart cowers
From the attachment of that one night
Now I smell his scent in a crowd
Now I think of him like a clown
Oh, Mother!
Shall we start yet another process to forget
No, he wants me not

That's My Mother

That's my mother
and
and I do not like how you treat her
and, sadly, I can't tell you, father
that I am not happy with how you treat my mother
because
because if I do
The elders will summon me
elders, who
treat their wives the same way, you
you treat my mother
and although dear father
I am happy with you as a father
I do not like how you treat my mother
unfortunately,
I cannot tell you because I am to be seen
not heard.

Eratso E. Noni

Song Of The Beauty

The song of the beauty, sparked my happiness
When I sing of you, I feel like some princes
I am the king, for that you love me,
In the deep sea, you evacuated me
You walk like a chameleon
Breath like a tree at noon, I can feel oxygen
Looking at your ant hills, make me unrest
Love touching them, when at rest
Come rejoice our love, the hawks have disappeared, see it?
Moon, stars, planets can witness us at night
Near the arrow house, looking in the sky
The moon dancing, the stars walking, we enjoy.
The song I sing, brightens my heart
You're on top of beauty, say you're cute
Smiling at me, double my span, as I laugh like a mad
Your teeth are better like that of a calf at sucking hard

Love my love, your first embrace made me mad.
Your second and third made me married
To the most beautiful of the land
Losing you, I can't withstand.
Sounds like a keyboard, giving the tune of blues
Sometimes I like when we are in chores
Taking you by hands, is like entering the Eden
Everywhere in the house I see your arts as you design
Entering the kitchen, oh! I am sorry
Plucking the chicken, woow! Don't worry

Let me do the rest, love is cooperation
Want to make ours the best, full of admiration
To you I am like a chick underneath your feathers
Protecting me against rainfall, sun rays and hawks
I am your umbrella; the sun can't harm you
The rain can't water you
The song of beauty, the song of your beauty
The beauty in you, makes me sing the song of beauty
I loved you, I love you, I will love you, love me, care me,
I will care for you
Not that I can live with you, but can't live without you
You're my brilliant beauty by nature
Good girl, sacred by culture
Love can withstand, love lasts
Love is nature, I love you.

Africa, My Africa

Work from the root, then stem, branches and leaves
Fight plunders, who reap from your shelves

Place to theirs, what wasn't meant for them.
Where are you, my Africa?
Don't ignore Mwajuma
For the sake of Monica
Kill not your men, knowing you're one
Dig the land more, dodge the trap, insufficiency.
Africa my Africa, protect the pumpkins, millet, palm
Africa my Africa, caress the groundnuts, sorghum
Africa my Africa, Make your soil, sands, of value,
Africa my Africa, Work from the root, that you be you.
Hear the songs, by the people of savannah
Songs from tropics, of great honour the luscious songs, not cloying the
ears
The heroic songs, giving out spears, don't ignore, drag into the mind
The medulla, front and back, don't blind
Africa, My Africa, hear the whispers, the songs.!
The lights from the hill illuminate
Let people run towards, they'll ululate
Pay heeds, how do they sound?
Song of the people, take the blind
Out of fire!
Steps ahead, protect the pearl
Larceny sniffing, be bold

Pen for pen, stick when in need
Detect your body, detect to threshold.
Table at table, tea to temperature
Collect the pebbles, picture them at future
Sons of the daughter and son, daughters of the daughter and son
Look at the beauty of savannah, at the sun, rainfall nourishing the land
Admired at eyes, main and the Island.
Can you hear the songs of your men?
Hear now, enclose them, fight the enemy by cane.
The hunter on trap, treat him as hunter, don't wonder

Um-huh! He is a poacher, take him, don't wander
The machines in operation
Making the beauty, for the children to live with commemoration
My Africa, plant more cereals -like rice
Don't forget to kill the mice and lice.
Think of you, think of the people
Refuse the refuse, you're not the cesspool
Sell the sales, buy the goods
Carry your luggage, your hands are safe
Blood flood is bitter, sight at it not
Be not a bat.

The Sleeping Bees

They buzzed, buzzed in a slumber
In them fresh as cucumber
To skunks, are blank slates
Memories demolished
Nothing to trace; that
Their honey was made out of bones and flesh
Blood, sweat, tears…
But now, the bees-drunk in sleep
Dozing off as hell.
The queen, the king
Now a house fly
Enjoying filths, leftovers
Hating hygiene and the rose aroma
Sniffing cadavers' scent
Betrayal! I don't know.
The sisimizi, the thieves, the skunks
Have put, beehive on a table
The glass tables
With plates to eat,
Knives to cut,
Forks to use,
Without water to clean hands
New ropes, new language, no idea!
Bees, vaguely napping, chewing at siesta, long sleep,

Do they care?
I doubt, is it real?
Do even birds trouble you?

Eat your honey and… Quiet?
Now the blackmailers
With venomous hot water, sneaking
Ready to thrash life, fearless of doom
A furtive move, grabbing honey, in their freakish hands.
Dear bees, where are your plans? Your tomorrow?
What'll your offspring cherish?
Beware, smuggling, sleep, weep you away,
Like sand on an undulating sea
On your feet bees, cast the snoring,
It's not too late.
RISE!

Energy Mavaza

Behind My Brows

Behind my brows are heinous scenes
Each blink am drifted in oblivion deep
In the fear archives within my genes
Appalling trepidations in my heart creep
Beaming vivid horror acts of slavery.

Behind my brows I hear black souls
Wailing ghastly in quandary state
Mothers nurse their toddler's sores
The custodians of the future's fate
Heavy load their tender shoulders bear.

Behind my brows I see dark images
Frantically wobbling under heavy wood
Whip driven further from their villages
Chained animals they're misunderstood
In the worst humanity servitude

Behind my brows fear hatchet, it bears
Lurks on nerves to murder my black ego

Maybe I'm the offspring feeble sires?
Or am the pious to white man's credo
Too scared in inferiority complex.
Behind my brows a distant flame glows
The rich jungle in between is my fear
Who will extinguish it when it's close?
Who will solicit loud that all can hear?

Who will unhinge the mind shackles bear?

Run Run Girl!

You made up your mind in vow,
To be control from hind like cow
On the yoke of matrimony
Like personalized slavery.
Bravery, tangled on your finger
Rage eating the edges of your anger
An eternal guardian, who,
Through dark and luck moments
Marks and keeps your comments
Bad or sad times he sticks like shadow
That disappears at night,
Reappears in the absence of fright
To lift your emotions to the greater height
So to skydive them, rock solid, to the ground.
Strong as he appears

He is impetuous like kids stir
Jumble of emotions in teacup.
Man up girl, man up!
Your feelings will splatter
On surface, on silver plateau.
Gather your pieces and run to fight later,
Those iron strong arms
Seldom hold hearts tender.
Run! run to the upheaved mound, shout!
Run girl run it's not your fault.

Harvest Of Thorns

That winters' sun shone so bright,
Thawed hearts in melanin delight.
Hope swallowed in ballot box,
Hope in Africa? What a paradox.
For nature nurtures its own well.
It adorns wild peppermints with green,
Climbers scale up rocks and boughs
Embracing the bush to keep the axe at bay.
Landscape painted in scattered thistles
In gloom-bloom as they shudder
To the August gust.
The firm rooted tastes November dew.
Thistles appease in summer breeze,

Whispering dry rumours to the prickly leaves.
Roots ferret beneath for moisture
But the ancestors stare licks our hope up.
Zealous ploughers did much about nothing
Silos awaited nocuous for stores but
Dust, the response to what we sowed,
Shrubs and thorns too.
No one knows what they fed on

We will reap what we did not sow
Bountiful harvest of thorns
We didn't toil for.

Aisha Naise Ahmad

The Pure Test

I wanna narrate a story
Also, I wanna portray
To portray the one and only.

The pure test
The story about....
The pure test!

The pure test brings development
To the nation
Fight against corruption
Also, it's a weapon
Against gender discrimination.

The pure test can change the world
It is the source of wisdom
It is the root of freedom.

Pure test is the key to success
Pure test gives the light
Now what is the pure test?

My mama once told me
The roots of pure test are bitter
But the fruits of pure test are sweeter.

You're My Catalyst

You're my catalyst
You speed up my reaction
Reaction of my attention
Attention towards my affection.

You're my catalyst
The first and the last
Just come close
I wanna give you a rose
A rose from where the sun rises.

You're my catalyst
You control my heartbeat
I enjoy dancing to your twists
Your happiness is my wish.

Dear catalyst
Your shining face
Makes my heart race
I'll always follow your pace.

Dear catalyst
Am not like Peter
Who follow you in Twitter
But am a promise keeper
And a real suitor.

Since you came into my life

I behave as a man having a wife
Always being wise,
Caring you more than thrice
Now let me confess to you
That,

For the first time we met
You we tiny little star
But now,
You're my whole universe
Yes,
You're my whole universe

Unforgettable Human

Brave than a man
The first one
To take the throne
The throne of a man.

Unforgettable human
Brought diplomacy
Diplomacy and democracy
This human can also sacrifice
Sacrifice anything for the seek of people's life.

Unforgettable human
Human who is multitasking
Also, who is on trending
Trending with not an ending.

Unforgettable human is a gift
A gift from creator
This human act as a mother
A mother and a protector
A protector and advisor.

Do you know this unforgettable human?
Let me give you a hint
A hint with the quiz
The quiz with the hint
This human is a mother, is a wife
But famously is a commander in chief.

Carolyne M. Acen (Afroetry MA)

50 YEARS LATER

(For Uganda on Independence Day)

We hoist our illusion
of freedom and chant
the colonialists' hymn.
We dramatise George Kakoma's
soliloquy on desperate
streets with hollow bellies.
Call the Oracle of the
bush war.
Then replay ironies of a virgin
Uganda in the bedroom
of the British Protectorate.
We claim freedom with
shackles on our feet.
We declaim yesterday's
atrocities at the sight of
the dying sun.
Divided we are.
Intolerant to each other.
Tribalistic and filled
with animosity.
58 years ago.
The union jack was lowered
and the Uganda flag was
elevated amidst excitement.
Our artefacts decorated

Kololo airstrip as we converged
to listen to a gleaming ambitious
Dr. Milton Obote.
Yes! Hope painted our faces.
Freedom buzzed around
like bees.
But are we worthy of this
bowl of adulation?
Yes! 58 years later.
We play history's plaintive
tone as a celebratory hymn
on 9th October.
Corrupt bellies take the
charlatan's script and
invite us to March.
We roast last month's
meat, and make merry
on the soil we have degraded.
We rhyme...
"Oh Uganda, the land that
feeds us" while our children
scavenge for food.
Bow our heads and praise
the oppressor.
Nod to the dictator in
a farmer's hat.
Priestly sermon of an
"Independent Uganda".
Clap and cheer.
Cheer and clap.
Yeah...we know.
You changed the locks
of Uganda in 1986
and swallowed the keys.

Clap and cheer.
Cheer and clap.
We wear the colonialist's
coat and March to a
beatless drum.
Colorful parade.
Free at last!
Brie, please.
No, Nile Special beer.

The Gospel According To Colonialism

The colonialists came
with a rifle and a Bible.
Taught us how to
pray with our
eyes closed.
To a God who hates
our dark skin.
While they stole our land,
plundered our resources
and degraded our once
rich soil.
Years later.
We raise the colonial Bible
higher than our conscious
minds.
We condemn and curse
in the name of White Jesus
with the patches of indolence
on our clothes.
We still pray with our eyes closed
while investors buy and
till our lands.
We have more Churches
preaching about prosperity
to a flock of sheep waiting to

be sheared in the rainy season.
We wail and wringe out our
eyes like sponges to an
unseen God while our
gardens remain unattended to.
The colonialists' religion
confused us.
Made us slaves in our lands.
The African proudly waves the
Bible like he wrote it.
Interprets the Bible in
the language of our ancestors.
Preaches like he was
St Paul.
Baptises like John the Baptist.
And embodies the stigmata
like the transfiguration was
made just for him.
The African wears the saintly
Church relic, breaks bread
and shares wine after the
liturgy and hopes
that he too will be beautified.
We are still latrines of
colonialism.
Products of a transgression.
Solving every problem
with religion.
While our children beg
on the streets,
and aspire to be preachers
and prophets.
Just like us.

Dark Skin Blues

"You look pretty for
a dark skin woman".
He blatantly said.
The din inside my head
subsided.
Beads of pain dripped
from my skin.
The universe crooned the
penitentiary blues while
the bleached sun looked on.
I felt the whips my ancestors
took descend on my tired back.
Shackles around my feet
rattled and I started choking
because of the heavy iron
collar around my neck.
Archetypes of my history
beamed on my charcoal skin.
Once again, I was on the
21st Century auction block
with my conscience stripped
and humiliated.
Perched in front of the new
age slave master who
flaunted the cowhide skin
of my kin.
Pride wept and the abrasions
of colorism sentenced me to

a hypovolemic shock.
The words sent a wave of
anger through my body.
I felt what Sarah Baartman must
have felt when she was being
paraded through the freak shows
in Paris and London.
The noose around my neck
tightened and the bough broke.
I felt so ugly in the midst of
the hegemonic depictions of
my identity as an African woman.
Pretty for a dark skin woman.
Fucking pretty for a dark
skin woman.
If it should be a curse,
a plague or a whiff of dust
in your tiny mind.
Let me flicker with the shadows
on the wall.
Roam this earth at 3 am like
a vile creature.
Haunt your enslaved mind
until your insecurities bleed out
of the incisions on your skin.
For I am the root of life's
genesis.
The original African Queen.

Tryphena Yeboah

Mama

She always seemed very harsh, impatient,
her judgements quick to be fired over everything—
when we spilled juice on a white tablecloth,
when we chewed too loudly or stained our mouth with soup:
"Your blindness has ruined my dinning cloth!"
"All that machine noise coming from your mouth,
there must be a grinder behind those teeth!"
One must not laugh or bow their heads in shame.
We shifted in our seats and remembered our manners,
but we also got used to it, and expected her voice
to come piercing through our days.
There were times we were fearless and gave no thought
to what she would do—in those moments,
we were too reckless, too clumsy, too foolish
to chase each other, or climb up a coconut tree,
our soft palms bruised from the rough barks.
We fell, scraped the skin off our kneecaps,
sprained our ankles and limped for days.
We were spanked, made to eat our dinner cold,
and watched the town games from the window.
We couldn't ask to join the crowds.
Once, we pretended we were saving swans on the lake
and nearly drowned—our small hands flailing,
our screaming voices breaking with panic, burning our throats.
Two strangers heard us, found us beating the surface of the water

and pulled us out. Dripping wet and cold, we were handed to her.
She collected us as if we were lost treasures, saying thank you, thank you,
and kissed the top of our dirty, soaked heads.
That night, she hummed and got to work quickly—
a cold towel on my brother's head for his starting fever,
a cotton dabbed in gentian violent over the cut above my eye.
We winced and waited for her to strike, yet her soft hands,
longing for what she'd almost lost, stroked us tenderly to sleep.

Coping Mechanism

One would expect me to withdraw,
or fling my hands up and weep in surrender.
Or worse, slam a door shut and throw myself
on the bed, defeated, afraid and in hiding.
It is the way of things, after all:
our emotions, a child's outburst—
careless, inconsiderate, and fickle.
I know this moment, too, shall end.
Because I have convinced myself that to love you
is to love all of you and in all seasons,
I head for the kitchen and pull out the pans.
I will make your favourite dish.
I will strike down the ends of these green beans,
I will press into and peel the skin off these potatoes.
Here is garlic to be crushed, onions to be pinned down and
sliced in perfect halves from the sharpness of this knife.
Remember my hands this way:
Setting the table, bringing food,
moving through this clumsy dance
of who's right and wrong
to touch the shy eyes of hunger.
You might join me in surrender or avoid me in shame.
But tonight, there will be the uneasy silence of quiet rage
and there will be something sweet to taste.
Between us, a distance stretches across the table
that is both strange and familiar.
Even as I sit here,

my finger on the spine of the fork,
your eyes lowered on your plate,
I know you are sorry,
but forgiveness will take its time.

Ronald K. Ssekajja

Convulsions

For the past 30 years,
Mother has been playing Aces
With the jackals of death.
Intoxicating her liver and kidney
With crude liquor with reckless abandon

For the fifth time,
I watch my mother bargain with death
The hospital now a mile away
My hands struggling the steering wheel
Convulsions becoming metaphors
She cannot disassociate from

Aback my car, my sister's eyes
A pool of wet pads
Despair and Pain, a make-up
They can't wash-off

Mother struggles
The blood out of her mouth
Soaks on the car seat,
Easily and perfectly
It's a sad art of paint and dye!

I ask God
Not to give me another sad story
To write about

Shadow Hunters Of My Joy

For the 20th time, I made a visit to the physician
showed her the bumper sticker;
screaming my vitals after lab technicians bleeding my veins.
Hoping she would finally accept that I need a physio-therapist
But she says no one needs to hear the grief within my bones
That there is no phone booth in the ligament of my body
And the whole world is dancing in the streets where I am broken
That I only need a psychotherapist and not that physio-therapist
To load out my pain to a deaf ear with pretty smiling lips.
Preaching to me that everyone finds happiness
If they care more about what they give than what they get.
And that my head should stop flying away
in chase of whirlwinds that have long vanished away
But these are my bones,
rattling to the days when the skies still spell my name.
But these are my bones,
The things I blame
When I can't get myself out of the bed.

But these are my bones,
They are what is broke
when the heart is long torn into pieces.
So, my hands are holding tight to the wounds of my hope
Trusting no one with the flexuous line of my spine.
Wondering what I need to swallow
To keep a thousand emotions down my throat.
Hoping that it will all get better
When operating theatre lights cleanout
the darkness inside my rib cage.
That my life would find light in the pulse of the stethoscope
Give strength to the Chandaria of my health
that has for long been hanging on a thread.
But if the worst day is still coming
I will still be here,
dancing in the beat-less song of loss
amidst needles and hospital bedsheets.

Flickering Moon

The Moon
has been flickering out like
an unshielded candle.

My prayers traffic lighted
Red
as the porch light in her eyes
beg that it's not just poetry
that spills from my mouth.

But all the verses
of my poetry
are shaped like a wedding cake.

The curl of her smile
an open church door
that history forbids us to enter.

But it's the look in her eyes,
the look in her eyes,
that bleeds my heart.

Jeresi Katusiime

Mother's Pride

My mother is proud
I scrub her pans
I tend her flowers
I sit and listen
To her stern warnings
Concerning the spreading of my legs.

My mother is proud
You can read it in her smile
As she presents me to church folk
'Nina is finishing her bachelors…'
She whispers loudly
To Ma Nam whose daughter
Is boiling Haj Hassan's potatoes.
I bundle my shawl
In front of my bloating stomach
My loose kitenge curtaining me
I have three more months
Before my mother's pride is diluted
Into a tasteless brew of shame

Will my mother be proud if she learns that
I have scrubbed her pans
Alongside musa's?
I have tended her flower bed
As I pruned Musa's?
I didn't only listen to her
Stern warnings concerning the spreading

Of my legs,
Musa taught me how
They must be spread.
Hopefully,
Mother will be proud.

For The Child Who Was Never Made

You are welcome.

Birthdays would have been bloodbaths
As you watched
A grown man and your mother
Search for a handle to fly off.

You would have had the best education
In 'Never compromising who you are'
As you watched mama
Master that Art.
Daddy
-well daddy
Would be daddy
Boys are always boys.

Your esteem would have been punctured
By your first cry for the attention

You would slice your wrists trying to get

Do I regret?
Not allowing you
To be made?

No.

You are welcome.

Do Not Tell My Husband

That I am a mother
Not a well of IQ
That everybody that squirms
In my amniotic fluid
Is bound to share a little of 'my brains'
A 'half of my cunning'
Three quarters of 'my charm'
And a full serving of 'my wit'

You
Caress gourd upon gourd
Reduce yourself to a shell of your former glory
Perfect the fine art
Of whisking skirts up

Sowing seed and blaming the garden
If its seedlings are full of weeds

This man calls me wanton and foolish
-He may be right
But whatever curtains veiled my eyes have lifted
He
-in his flaming wisdom
Should have clung to his mother
If he wanted an IQ well
To carry his offspring.

Reluctance throbs in my veins when I lean on him

The caution of an asthmatic man
Saturates each breath
This man
-mother says
Is just a man.

Carla-Ann Makumbe

Awaiting You

Awaiting you is the wind that blows announcing
the rains
It is the scent that prepares my senses of our
evolving.
It is the skipping of an excited kid as she
goes home
where a warm meal awaits.
It is the first sunray that breaks after floods.
Awaiting you are the expectations running in my
mind.
It is the intensity passed between our looks
and the smiles
warming my heart.

It is the lightness of having your shoulders and
being protected by your embrace.
Awaiting you is the remedy to all my doubts, it is the
firm grip you give as you whisper in my ear
"I will not let you go."

As She Is

There she goes,
Rising again from the ashes like a phoenix once again!
There she goes,
Owning her nine lives call her Cat Mother.
There she goes,
Fixing the crown on her head as she heads back into the fire, an Amazonian goddess.
There she goes,
Heart in shards whilst tongues are sharpened and pointed and her so when hell breaks
loose,
Their shards sink into her heart, and she falls.
Legs first, hoping the clouds will catch her and let her float in their embrace before she
has to try again.
Yet there she finds herself,
Lying in blood dripping from her skin as the veins give in and all she gets are jeers as she
is exposed, no tree to hide behind and once again like hungry vultures they pounce on her
very soul.
No bush to cower under,
Just her and my crown with each other's backs.
There she goes,
Walking proudly where she is expected to tiptoe,
And defying these flaws that have been made to dishearten her.
There she goes,

Walking on these eggshells and making them tarmac for generations to come.
There she goes,
Breaking barriers and hurdling over biases!
There she goes,
With her weaknesses laid bare and their shards continue to shoot,
She stands petrified, heart crushed as blood shot eyes give her relief,
And so there she stands,
Crown of thorns adorned, blood dripping she reflects the Saviour as this crown wears
her.
Here she is,
Laying it all bare for the world to dissect.
Here she is,
Still smiling as more than once labels have been stuck on her forehead.
Here she is,
Proclaiming she came, she saw, and she conquered.
Here she is,
Black woman come to perch on this view at the top like as eagle.
Here she is
Still winning and blowing smiles to faces, gracefully with strength of a fairy godmother.
Here she is,

She'll let us in even though knives have been twisted, that's love!
Here she is,
Standing by the thing we sought to hurt her with tossed and broken,
Still standing,

Still believing,
Still reaching for the stars!
There She Glows, call her a proud black woman.

We Are

We are statistics
We are numbers stamped on foreheads and knees
Suffocating from their hands imprinted on our necks.
We are colour coded, given affinities of darkness and
some privileged man stabbing our souls as we explode
into nothingness.
We are the cries of mothers as our wombs weep.
We are the algorithm they couldn't figure out, so we keep
being trampled on by
stampedes.
We are George Floyd wailing on the tarmac as death
seduces him.
We are the numbers in Zimbabwe reaching for hope as
we are devoured by "freedom."
We are the graduates in Nigeria turning to blood as it
begins to fill the pockets.
We are the shacks in the depths of South Africa as this
jungle swallows our hope.
We are in shackles with chains dangling, will the sun heal
our souls.
We are poverty personified as ours leaves no colour.
We are of lost souls on foggy nights as leaders turn blind
eyes.
We are shot when the speaking starts and shut down
when thinking calls.
We are at no man's land as we take all blows and it all
comes down to,

We are a people enslaved by lack of change and we are the cactus in the desert.
We are the stench in the wind as we wail like banshees for our futures to be appeased.
We are generation where money has been talking for decades so the truth long since took a walk.

Jasper Harry Sabuni

Does It?

Does it make me an African
since I adhere less to time,
A habit and defect
vaguely believed to be inherited
and culturally embedded deep within our DNA?
Does it make me less of an African
since I herded no cattle back in the days,
But instead, I had a dog by my side
cuddled her on my lap
while playing with a tag on her neck
written BANTU her name?
Does it make me half African
that I am fluent in the white man's language,
I'm entirely competent in English
and well conversant in French,

But still…

I can't go beyond "The Greeting"
for I know less of Chasu, my mother tongue?
Does it make me an African
just because I'm Black!
But does this make him, Barack,

Once deemed to be the world's most powerful black man,

Does this alone make him African

even though he's nothing black on the inside?

Well, if it does…
That's absurd!

Does it mostly make me an African
due to the fact that
I was merely born in this continent?
But what about Britty?
A lady friend of mine born, in Bulgaria,
But she's most passionate at heart
'bout Africa than I and the most of us,
Doesn't that qualify her to be African?

Does it make me not an African,
Since I know none of the dances of Makhiriri,

But I could actually
protest with words and in rhymes,
Through hip hop and poetry,
From abroad via the waves,

On the unjust and unfairness acts of our Serikali?

Does it make me an African
That I read most of…

Chinua Achebe's, Wole Soyinka's, Elieshi Lema's
Shaaban Robert's, Ayi Kwei Armah's, Grace Ogot's literature!?

But still…

I'd fancifully live a lucrative and extravagant life

contrary to Mwalimu Nyerere's Lectures on Ujamaa?

Does it make me not an African
since I cannot tolerate
the idiocy and mediocrity of the elders,

When they go astray,
But I'll still greet them SHIKAMOO
as I do not fancy the white man's Hello!
Does it make me an African

That I adore, love and actually do feel comfortable,

When and where I wear
the beads, cultures and batik on my body,
But would still be ashamed

of dressing so in front of the UN General Assembly?
Does it or doesn't it make me an African,
When I question whether or not I'm an African,

When I question whether…
I am more, less, somehow an African!

If I Die Today

When I inhale my last breath
and my soul departs
bidding farewell from this universe,

I insist...

You withhold your sentiment,
Spare me your dissent
and your obscenely vile
so full of disgust,
If I die today…
Terrorize not my past,
Of what will be the essence
to stain my corpse?
If I die today,
Indeed, ignore my vices,
Uphold my virtues,
Undo my plights,
If I die today…
Applaud my doings
But not in excess,
Highlight my misfortunes
and realise its lessons,
If I die today,
Let I die indeed,

Resurrect I not back from the dead,
If and when I die,
Let I die and rest at ease.

Silence

Condemn my silence,
It irritates,
It resonates,
It disturbs,

Its echo disrupts their attention,
It holds them in contention
not knowing what exactly are my thoughts,

Anxiously they await,
That moment…
I'd open my lips
I'd awake from sleep

and unveil myself from the mute sheets,

Condemn my silence,
It disturbs their peace
It alters their tranquillity,
But I caution you this…
My voice!

Its sound is of no benevolence!

Nicole Natsai Chimanikire

It's Raining Today

It's raining today
I wish I could rain too
I wish I wasn't like the rain but was the rain
I wish I was nourishment
A prayer answered
An ancestral beat of patience
A story too enticing to just be beautiful
I wish I came with lightening
I wish the earth cracking was my theme song
An interlude to beauty and grace
I wish everyone made space when I came through

The rains

oh, they make me believe that God loved us at some point.
And they make me remember he couldn't stand us at other points

Remember Noah's ark?
I know.

I know he promised he'd never destroy the earth with water again
But…. Correct me if I'm wrong Chimanimani is a part of the earth right.

It's an actual place right, with people right,

Where are they now and…. Where was he?
These types of questions make honesty a harsh argument.
Let's focus on the fact that it's raining today
Is it washing away the past?

Or

is it sinking in the present?
Is it making rivers or flooding them?
Is thunder music?
And if so what genre?
Because sometimes
Symphonies

and other times it's a hard metal band the type that doesn't get paid

Emotionally Numb

I've been emotionally numb for seven days
Don't ask me how I got here

Don't ask me what plans I have to get out of the mental void space that has a hold me

Don't ask,

Don't ask me questions I can't answer

I've tried.
But

It's just the same as listening to a song, the words are there, hanging in the air, but.... In four
different languages all of which I don't understand, two of which don't exist and one of which was
lost to the ages of slithering serpentine suspended systems of a back brace that can't sustain itself.
This is the stain that spread across the district, markings of a woman taken by the wind.

So again, don't ask me how I got here

It honestly wasn't my own doing, I was kidnapped by failure, somehow ended up in fears arms, you could say I've got Stockholm syndrome because well I somehow fell for him or fell into him, no

Difference
really.

We've got two kids now. My first-born son anxiety and
my dear daughter depression. We are trying
for a THIRD! although he doesn't know it yet, I'm already pregnant, I already know her name, her

names hope.
Fear is not her father.

Unlike in most relationships this time it didn't end like
this because he didn't give me attention no it's a result of
all the attention.

So again, don't ask me what my plans to get out of this
space are
I already got myself knee deep in dark thoughts venturing out to find hope

She Came Out Of The Sand Of Time

She came out of the sand of time
Woven into grace and grandeur
She called every inch of space
her body contained
a home.

She was house, stone of ages, promises of love and understanding
She was a mountain, a steady sign of sovereign splendour

She was a war
a fight of eagles and doves
a battle of leopards and lions
She was an anomaly.

It is hard too hard to understand what nature created so perfectly

And she is perfection

For the moment eyes take comfort in her presence
it is apparent, blatantly clear that
she is a story with lines everybody
wants to read.

That if anyone should fall for the stars, they would land in her eyes

For she is the only being that made mountains out of molehills, came crashing but bore the force of

gravity

Turned tragedy and calamity into an aim and that aim into an outcome and in that outcome came

the glory.

She rose out of the sand of time

A back brace to a race that at times turns their back on her

But she is Woman
Her voice is the roar of thunder for she rose out of the sand of time

Justine Nagundi

The Sulking Son

Weep not Child
What is not yours is not yours
Things fall apart
The sands of time
Becoming
Echoes of tired men.

One day I will write about this
Place– all the bright places.
Everything I never told you
Becoming
The magic of ordinary days.
Normal people
Becoming
Brave not perfect.
Half of a yellow sun
Becoming
A thousand splendid suns.

The Eternal Noon

The strange cat leaps
And stops mid pounce
See the frenzied flight
Of the frozen dove!

A shoeprint etched in wet tarmac
A filthy beggar with a swollen hand
Brings a new bronze coin
To his pointed mouth.

For one hour it has been
One minute to noon.

The sly wind lifts her skirt
And holds it up
See the tattooed frowns
And lolling tongues.

See the whole world stop
While she gnashes her teeth
See her strike a pose
And she bleeds and bleeds…

Lessons In Womanhood

'Men want a woman
As immaculate as a church'
Men love to wonder
What's in her strained glass

Men draft long statutes
Defining mini skirts.
Men draw the line
Between sexy and slut.

'Men adore ladies
With shy, tinkling laughs'
Men crave our cousin
Who knows all the bars.

If men love a creature
Who's all the above.
Then women must try harder
To give less of a damn.

Fungai Gwen Makuyana

In The Shadows

right after the burial of her son
Maita lost her voice
she didn't eat or sleep
she simply spent the day
starring in the shadows
her husband said he was tired
her grief denied him of his wife
and when her in laws returned her
all that she had left were
photographs
of her child
and memories
a small toy
sitting on her dresser.

'she barely speaks'
they said
she, a motherless child
she, a childless mother
the epitome of grief itself

I Loves You, Porgy...

(After Nina Simones Ballad)

This is how every record speaks my heart to you
Listen to my heartbeat in the dark calm spaces between
Nina Simone's ballads
Trace my story in the curves of her heavy notes and soul
My affection for music is beyond a love affair
Its how to speak a broken tune so perfect it's a melody
And if you ever need to speak your heart out that way, just know
I love you

How They Made Her

Amai is not satisfied
until she has made
everything from scratch
with her bare hands.

Most of it is time
spent keeping busy
and the skill
is most necessary
for as long as
it fetches her a dollar.

She be mother China
with untiring hands

to lend and keep,
her back is the bone
of everyone who
knows her.

Amai says idle hands are
the devil's workshop
and she be the closest
thing to God.
So she mends broken things.
She rebuilds relationships.
She is weaved by the blood
Of her mother, and her mothers

Before her.

She be something defiant
Ripped out of a forgiving
womb. A child of wisdom.
And resilience. Strength.

Elizabeth Kayongwe Lukoma

Lies He Told

When I was twelve, I left home and never looked back.
My story became a tale, a tale that was whispered but never told.
They remembered but couldn't say my name.
They said, 'ikwo,' that girl can't be mentioned, it is forbidden!
But how could they say that it is their guilt that chocks them in between the tale?
So they wait for one who tells it best without guilt,
The staggering old woman whose skirts spoke of war and nails that scribbled death,
With yellow eyes that see beneath skin, she saw it all.

She says, 'ikwo,' it is I, leaving wasn't a choice!
The first time he came to me, I was ten; my breasts had just started pointing sharply to the north.
He said, 'ikwo,' you have ripened; he pulled at my breast.
I could think it was a cat that was licking my face; he smelt of cheap brew.
It was said that he never had money to pay for anything in the village.
But I couldn't scream or speak, how could I?
I had never said a word since my birth; my papa and mama said I didn't cry.
His hands left an ache all over; I called his fingers dirty.

He came back on the eve of my twelfth year; I was sleeping in his hut,

My dear uncle's hut! 'ikwo,' it is time, he said.
His rough hands willed the strength out of my neck.
He acted like a cat again, licking off the dirt on my skin;
my stomach almost let go of my
Supper.
He raised my rebellious skirts as he struggled to lose his
tattered trousers.
When I felt the pain, it is then that I screamed.
He left me, told all the villagers I have let all the fisher-
men in between my legs,
& 'ikwo,' I couldn't handle the disappointment in my
people's faces.

I left on my twelfth year.

The dirty scary medicine woman took me in, pushed
rotten banana down my throat
& 'ikwo,' you need your voice… She pushed more.
So when the rains fell and the ground was smooth, she
rested.
I buried her in the thick bushes and took her place.
My breasts had long fallen, my skin had long roughened,
And my will has since gone to rest.
'ikwo,' you still can't mention her name.
She was a bird that wasn't meant to find rest.

Redeem

This is to men,
To a generation of men that imitates fathers' thoughts in pretense
To a generation that kills its first born
To one that rapes its own words
To that that will forget to maintain their lie the next second.
To men who love going beyond their heads,
To men who assume responsibility to relationships they haven't started.

But this is also to ladies,
Ladies not girls, those who sell themselves cheap,
Those who allow to constantly be rubbed against the wall,
Those who let their insecurities torture them,
Those who sell themselves to relationships that don't exist.
A relationship that has not been formed
This is to girls who tear out their hearts for men who do not want them.

This is no poem,
This is a painful sour reaping from my midnight nightmare
To how fast this generation of men has assumed,
When he says hello, the next day he wants you to warm his bed,

Better yet he has earned himself a laundry lady.
The great ulcer that has consumed them and mists their faces,
So damning that the dirty mist has spread to the eyes of my gender,
That you keep grasping onto a relationship that is fiction.

Today Was

The skies were blue yesterday,
The birds hovered ceremoniously in a pattern as the wind picked up blowing the smell of
cheap meat to her nostrils
She enjoyed the scent slowly taking a sip from her red stained glass as she pitched her nose,
raising her radio to report the kill and thrill
The thrill of having to kill the hope of the future that stared at her with red teary eyes of hope
and trust.

The children huddled into the murk of their mother's petticoats, shivering as they watched
her stumble over their neighbours.
The boy under his father's coat murmured in shaking tones wishing he had been exported for
labour.
He scarcely noticed the choked sob that his mouth expelled,
Life had been good, he thought.

Across him in the village street lay the pieces that once connected him to the sunshine,
The sun she was as she balanced the brown port on her head.
He thought of how they had danced in the rain as the soft drops penetrated their coats,
Chilling them to the bone but yet warming them up.

Who was to warm him now as he shivered with the longing of his bed that lay scattered as a
fire starter where his father's head rested?
He heard her chuckles as she walked by, her brown boots discoloured with wet red stains.

Today as the moon sailed out, fresh tears slid down his cheeks as the struggling lump in his
heart made him numb.
He is being taken away!
He thinks he won't be changed by what the future holds,
He is sad he won't know where to lay his flowers in future to remember them.
As she approached, He picked a small white stone that has been painted red and stares.
One day he would pass through as he fought her wars.

Will he remember that he once hated who did this to him, will his friends remember?
Or will she blind him with the redemption tale and make him forget his ancestors.
Today there was smoke over the horizon. There was only one sound
The sound of birds feeding on the ground as their claws dripped in blood!

Emestina Edem Azah

Chestgrow Things

We're calling out
All the beasts in our wild.
Let them come for us.
This flock of sheep/ too tired
Of being fear/ of hiding.
No more.
Drawing blood you will take anyway,
If we will perish, then you must too. We will rinse out your existence from our memories. We
will die happy, never haven known you.

You swore yourselves protectors—but no.

What does a bruised sky look like?
Is it bloody or a sky raining blades?
When pain descends in the morning, like fog so dense we can't see each other, we scream!
Because you wash your dirt on our food in our faces and push it down our throats.
Because our lungs are on fire and we're humans nomore only bodies and bones that'll decay.
Because we hold broken shards tightly and our wounds hurt but we don't let go.
We're screaming our guts out to protect the shards from air.
These same shards pierce us to protect themselves.
And we, wondering where the blood in our bodies went,
Why the warmth left,

And why we cry no more.

Help Me Sound Like Heaven Or It's Stairway So I Can Be Close To You

God,
I wish I could pray like my neighbour, with more sincerity.
It trembles in her voice/ her pleas to you to keep her family safe and kind and happy.
I try/ but my voice quivers / I don't want to make a lot of sound when talking to you/ I don't
want to be a pharisee/ but isn't telling everyone that you know God a kind of sincerity/ a vow
to uphold him no matter what/a singling to follow the straight and narrow path?/ But my
breathing shakes my prayer up, liquifies it into my eyes and makes it sound like soup boiling
on the stove.
I hear the churches in the area pray and sing till their loudspeakers carry their voices to
heaven./ Because for them, you only appear in the night on certain days. And if they don't
shout enough, the night will drown their voices in the stars, and they'll remain impoverished
because your ears were too far.
I don't know if sincerity has ever belonged in my prayers. I can hardly pray without

remembering the format.
First gratitude
Then numerous pleas
Then I end in the name of Jesus.
But I crave a friendship and a solitude that is us.
Me and you.
Only us.

States Of Matter; A Human Being Can Be Transmuted When They Are Suffering And Still Exist.

Something hurts in my body.
I don't know what it is,
Not yet.
It hurts in various places/It sears up my insides.
I can smell burning flesh in my thoughts, and I know it's me.
It's me that's burning but I don't know exactly which part is burning.
I don't know how to turn off this thing causing me to hurt, but I feel my body breaking down.
My skin is doing her best to hold me together. She sees the wind as it flirts with the hair on
my arms/ she feels the world changing and she tells me we can change too/the fire will leave
and there'll be water/ but I can't see any of these. My head has been squeezed into a lead pot/
no matter how smart I am, I cannot see a solution without a depreciation. When I tell people
I'm tired, they think it's physical.

I'm beginning to become a pool of blood under my legs, and I'm the only one who can see it.
The world is full of water/Too much water and drowning is the only reasonable thing/so I
stay here because the water is warm and listens to me.
Maybe this is not drowning at all.
Maybe I just might have been wrongly prejudiced against water.
Maybe just shapeshifting/ form exchange.
Like in a myth./Because shape shifters are not real and nothing in this world is real now. At least not right now.
Then I can become water. Melting into the earth once I touch it, only
coming out occasionally to look at the colour of sky and go back.

Tatiana Natalie Kondo (banshee)

Enough

Your hips will fold
Your skin will un-mould
Your breast will fall further from your chest
And birth-giving marks on your waist, they will rest
But you will still be beautiful
You may even lose parts of you,
Your hair, your sight, your smile
But you will still be full and worth the while
You will still be worthy of all that he could not give you
You will still be you and that there,
That there is enough!

Salt

Those that do not lack,
Pierced the rainbow and it cried in black.
It poisoned the sea and made it salty and that is why we are bitter

Drowning

We are tired if drowning in debt,
Teach us how to swim,
Teach us how to keep our heads above the water we struggle in
So that we can see the sun as it rises again in the East,
Bearing our hope.
Throw in the rope,
So that we can be saved and start saving,
Enough for our future generations to float above the threatening tides of this landlocked nation

Oppong Clifford Benjamin

Everything Ends At Where Everything Starts

how do you
punish your
body?

do you
sit on the concrete floor
in a room of
morose darkness
and repaint losses
failures, bitterness,
disappointments, and rejections?

do you
scream in darkness,
do you slam a fist into walls,
do you think a demon lives
in your belly,
do you pinch your skin
till blood reminds
you that life is still in the
living?

most importantly

do you pay attention

to the elasticity of your body;
how it finally sighs,
calms itself and stands up,
walks to the switch to replace
darkness with light,
how your body discovers
home as though it never got lost,
as if you have always been home?

how do you punish
malleable objects;
how do you punish yourself?

The Building Is In The Reconstruction

when the rain falls

let it hit our windows sill
our noses acknowledge
the scent of the first earth
rising to freedom
our minds wishing to join the ascension.
and when the rain stops
the birds must be heard chirping
in the yellow atmospheres outside our room
rebuilding everything they lost in the waters,
a twig after twigs, a leaf after leaves,
with each step they take, they've arrived.

Choosing Colours For Destiny

fear grows in our bellies
when our mothers tell
the stories of our fathers

but they also say
kaftan is always sewn in plain colours
choose your colour as craftily
as birds build their nest,
as sands go up for the rains to come down,
as midnight silence in a dark room

when they are acting our story,
they must indeed say we tried
to be rainbows
but nature chose the colours

Billyhadiat Taofeeqoh Adeola

Paradise In Between My Thighs

You are a god;
everything you tread
becomes a stair towards your throne
and your words, like scriptures; a holy momento
that wakes the heart from eternal slumber.
So, allow me to worship you while I cry vowels
for my salvation with bent knees,
head bowed and arms unfurled
while you kiss me in the rain
under a blanket of shimmering
stars - You are a god!
O! How exalted are your names?
To your wake, flowers bloom.
Allow me to name you the lord of spring.
Or shall I blame you for the fall of leaves?
And if I come to you, falling, would you
catch me in your arms or like autumn leaves,
watch me plummet, rot and wilt?
You are a god—
Oh! Should I call you summer?
For you my heart burns
with you, darkness ceases to live
and my world, no longer monotonous.
You are a god,
In this hitched-up catastrophe,

Let my lullaby be the throbs of your heart
while I sing you a thousand songs
That my love be shown in every lyric
and its depth be felt in its rhythm
until my very last breath
and lay down with my sweet sorrows,
kiss me goodnight and clutch your hands around
me while you bring paradise onto my thighs.

Honeymoon Blues

Tonight, I crave not a blanket.
Pull me from the waves of rumpled bedsheets
And beach me on your body
For all I want is your warmth and sheer closeness.
Your dire touch and smell.
Tonight, no words.
Just silence and dim lights.
Our hearts will do the talking—we listen
As I stare into your eyes
For my desires are locked
and the key is in your gaze.
Tonight, make me your favourite flower.
Dance me around
And watch my veil fall like autumn leaves.
Tonight, own me forever
And strip me off my sanity
As we dive into this ocean of everlasting love.

This Is Not Love

Love is not you kissing
the scars you have etched
with slaps and kicks over spilt beer.
It's not you hugging me tight
to gather these pieces of my being
that you broke with hammering words.
Love is not you buying me makeups to mask
these colours on my face
that you splashed with the fury of your fists
and neither is it your thousand professes
of how much you do and will forever love me
to mute the yell of my heart with kisses
after I taste unfamiliar lipstick on your lips.
It's not you leaving like we never met
while I, under the spells of moonlight,
embrace you like you never left.
Love, my dear, is not healing from wounds
and then run back into those hands
that etched them on my skin.
Love is not death
and neither is it this
shackle you slid into my finger.

Nnane Ntube

Magical Pen

The
Pen
I had
last night
I didn't know
It was a Pen till
on my refined wood
began to flow, it flow'd
it flow'd a'd flow'd a'd flow'd
in my loneliness didn't stop to flow
And my silence gave it ease to flow…
As from my senses dug with ease to flow
To give a bright sense to my snowy world
I was glad to see it painting my holey walls
And the ease with which it colourfully did
Then with burning hope proudly said to me,
"I'll flow and flow… till the ends of the earth
if only… like an anchor you do hold me tight
And with me show the world the desir'd light"
With hopes so high, we smiled to let it flow…
Now we live in the light we share that flows.

Nothing Like A Kiss

Today,
I kissed a stranger
I kissed him
—and left with my heart gone

…I don't know…

for once I felt whole
though my heart was gone
—desires burn my lips
I have to fight against myself

why now? why him? Who's him?

Today,
I kissed a stranger
it came like a dream
I kissed him
—and killed my soul

…choking

'twas nothing like a kiss

The Wait

Like still water,
My bird and I gazed
As the moon puts on its shade
When the trumpet sounded 'corona'
And horizons broke through like dray
Chasing everyone away

My bird had yearned for the drey
To sing to little squirrels
While standing on the hay
And I have yearned for the bakery
To fill my raffia basket
While getting ready for the day

Like a bray, the news came:
"Coronavirus is on its way!"
My bird and I laid off,
Into the house we made our way.
But my bird flew and stood 25 feet away
Then we counted ticks of the clock:
Tic, tac, tic, tac…
Waiting for corona to go away

Philani Amadeus Nyoni
Three Sonnets

LXXIV

You uplift me, like the eastern horizon
That mothers the sun. You cloth me,
When the wind whips you are warm saffron.
You strengthen me; raise me from knee,
Put courage in heart and sword in hand,
Or a sling to fell the towering Goliath.
You calm my mind, when you understand
You part a mist from my mental labyrinth,
I am sane because you hear and believe
Despite what the world has to say.
You are a sunny cleft, by you I cleave
A spot of sunshine in any storm, any day.
I wrote this because something within insists
I should thank you, for the fact that you exist.

CLI

Speak not of love in times of war

When lovers' eyes bleed like battlefields
And shells ring like wedding chimes on church floors.
Speak of the night and naked heart that bleeds
On naked heart, thumping like a legion's march;
Eroding pleasantries, tramping roses planting fears.
Speak of silences echoing in the hust
Tones of love, speak oh love in crystal tears.
Speak of futures bleak in outlook but bright
In our hearts, we could leave it all behind
If we knew there was a piece of hope beyond night.
Close your eyes, speak in kisses for love is blind,
Speak not of love for tomorrow we die,
Speak of paradise inn which tonight we dine.

CCLV

It's a fucking lovely world in here.
The girl I want to marry just told
Me she spent the night in another man's lair.
So much for a heart of gold.
I spent the night watching the lights across
Wishing we had some to power up my machine
That hums like a refrigerator and cross
Over to my friends from the imagination.
She holidays in America, he's of wealth,
And I am just a sonnet-writing freak.
She'll write a book on when I leave earth.
I'm beautiful, she says, but doesn't wanna fuck.
I'll just keep writing until the heavens part
And God tosses me a dime for a cigarette.

Hauwa Shaffii Nunu

Fault Lines

because I am trying to hold
my brother's cracks together,
to keep him from falling
like a pebble into my shadow,
I walk in a zigzag in front of him for too long.
I forget to look back
because I know no other darkness but mine.
I protect him from no other darkness but mine.
so when he falls into a hole,
I don't see the pitch dark inside it as a thing
that is his, a thing that belongs to him.
my guilt is a room without air.

Prayer

every time I break skin to escape myself, it is a prayer rendered to blood. every time my heart widened
itself in love to a person, it was a prayer offered in defiance to order.
I am trying to say that the first time my father stood behind his son in prayer,
it looked a lot like absolution. the earth around them shifted into place.
it was a lifetime looking backwards, a sigh in reverse.
and how do you measure progress except to say it is happening differently?
the gap between them was sometimes water, sometimes a hole.
either way, it was a vicious mouth, gaping all the time.
in prayer, it could have passed for peace.
prayer held the gap between them and called it sacred. with the same mouth,
it swallowed it afterwards. it was mercy in a tongue that was also kind.
I have always known mercy to set out with a sharp edge.
that day, they shifted into new forms like angels trying out space.
in prostration, they were identical,
backs bent, an offering to god. standing and heads bowed,
they were a restitution. but foreheads to the ground, they became human and human,
father and son.

human and son, father and human.
human and human.

Prayers

I

eyes are not the window to the soul,
it's the hands.

II

the last day of ramadan,
I watch my brother recite his longest du'a
so far.
his hands cupped and held out to god;
take me as I am, take me.
it is a litany of everything
that has bared him roughly.
his voice—stripped of its deep timber—
is kneeling on its own.
in some verses, it is raw as a wound.
his voice weeps,
his shoulders quake with the weight
of these past years,

but it is his trembling hands that stay with me.

Esnala Banda

Inception

In the beginning, God created music.
He created my heart to beat in time to yours.
Can you hear that sound? Can't you hear our hearts resound?
In the beginning, I met your words.
They touched me before I met you.
I knew you before I touched you.
Tell me is this our start?
Is this the beginning of your purpose birthed at conception?
Push!
Give birth to your art like you received your life blood.
Push!
We are bound like the cord that led to conception.
Start!
Start at the beginning and walk towards your purpose.
Just start!
Start right at the end with your goal in hand until you reach it.
Start!
In the beginning, you had me.
Your mind met mine before my eyes saw you.
I couldn't stay caged because you tore through.
I tried to stay shackled, but who can ignore you?
You undressed my mind and crowned me with yours.
And in its nakedness, you found me.
Long before I found you, you found purpose and wrote the words I bathe in.

The words whose dregs I so willingly drown in.

So yes. Push!
Break all my boundaries and take more.
Push!
Ink your way into my timeline as sands run.
Push!
Let your words pin me into corners with no escape.
I have tasted your mind and willingly take it.
In the beginning, you gave me your words,
And so today, I give you mine.

Her Story - Flowers

Of all the things I've lost in life,
I value my tears the most.
In self-discovery, I've found that some tears ought never to leave their host.
So I'm done crying;
Crying over men with chips on their shoulders,
Whose only method of release was to break my porcelain heart into a million pieces,
Crying over men who broke my body just so they could attain an orgasm,
Crying over other women who still believe rape can only be as a result of the victim,
Crying over men who believe women are nothing but pleasure domes and so treat us as such.
In the bleakness of the gutter, my petals gather colour and courage daring to flower in the midst of
helplessness.
I understand now that the world has its own demons
And that sadly, most of them look like me and my kind, and so they treat all born with a womb as
accursed,
Even when you bear their likeness.
You tell me to take responsibility and change the way I dress.
All I hear you say is a man will never be made to learn to curb the chaos in his pants!
So don't blame the girls who think that love sounds like an opening zipper,

Or feels like unwelcome hands in nether regions if you won't show them any better,
Then get mad when they treat you how you treat them.
Just let my flowers bloom.
Roots digging deeper with every victim.
Our petals will blow free until women find a place to land.
If society won't grant me a safe haven, I will create one for my garden.
Our gender doesn't rank us in second place.
I have never known a womb to settle,
See the globe may scatter our petals but we are all blooming for the dame bouquet.
Hello, World! Today, I throw you her story.
You better catch it.

Future Love Letters

This is not a love poem.
It is a mere rearrangement of the alphabet with you at the centre.
I am not a lyricist so that was not a punchline,
I just want you to read between the lines and take what's yours.
Dear Future past,
I want to say I love you at every ticking tock and mean it
But I dare not because I know not how you will receive it.
And so the cycle continues;
Here today, Gone tomorrow,
Love today, forget tomorrow.
I miss you now as I will in future.
The reasons I love you outweigh the number of words that exist to convey emotion,
But still, I put my heart and soul into my words for you.
So that if ever I am gone, the ink will stay with you.
Knowing a soul like yours exists, that alone makes the possibilities of this world infinite.
So today I love you in analogue with pen to paper, ink to nib.

Your soul plunges mine into orbit,
You possess such a light that my being cannot but male revolutions around you.
I could call you a star but that is both a cliché and an understatement.

You are a wielder of galaxies with a voice that echoes in the silence,
Leaving darkness, no chance to hold its fear.
You are some kind of royalty with a copper crown,
Some kind of ruler on a lover's throne
Surrendered hearts bow to you in enthralled awe.
As tribute I put my pen to paper and watch it bloom,
Letting my love be watered by ink and faith.
I love you with the intensity of a thousand fires and you are my kindling.
A much-needed want, and a most cherished craving,
That beautiful light between night and day.

Zziwa Zinbala

I Meant, He Is Gay Not Gay

I meant, he is gay not gay.
I met a gay person,
With a gay smile.
His friendship was gay
But gay!

(He tried to say, do not fear me. I love boys but we can still be friends.)

I met a gay person,
With a gay smile.
He loved women like sisters
That. Their petite bosom
Make him uncomfortable and envious.
He craves for a big bottom.

(He said, I want it gigantic. Didactic to anyone that I am gay but gay.)

I met a gay person
With a gay smile
He offered solace
Solely, his soul was divine.

(He said, I feel I am comfortable being female. I just
want strip dance for my husband. I am gay.)

I met a gay person,
With a gay smile.
I unblotted my feelings,

Tried to muster energies
Garner support and love
But I failed to welcome him.

(He said, we can still be friends, right? I kinda feel lonely.
I feel the world toppling on my shoulders. I
need a person to talk with.)

I met a gay person,
With a gay smile.
He was lost about his sexuality
I was straight about mine.
I love my women with –
Big eyes, curvy hips, slender waist
And eyes that smile
With voices deeper!

***

He loved his men
With big pencils
Budging triceps and biceps
And taller necks
With deeper voices
And beards.
He loved his men dark skinned.
Unlikely I was short and brown,

Beardless and confused.
I thus escape the woos of his charms.

For Richer, For Richer

To dust doth returned was made for man
But
For richer, for richer
Even in death the rich wins...

At his lavish wedding, I recall
We eat to full
The cuisine was perfectly the finest
We feasted like royals
And dined with kings
We drunk our hearts out
Danced to his tunes
He was never funny, but he was a lavish giver.

Our rich in the hood is dead!
The ding dong
The gong banging
The siren of his death
Mounted our village
We were numb with the news.
I recoiled and coiled
He was the backbone of our community
He was educating my children
Sad!

For his coffin was made of the finest oak tree

It was polished lavishly with a brown colour

I mirrored myself at the brown and fixed my necktie
The white cushions resting his dead head
The suit, hmm!
For richer, for richer.
Even in death the rich still wins

I then gazed upon the multitude that came to mourn his passing
The condolences in millions
My heart craved for only a tenth of it. My children needed school fees.

I looked at his grave being molded in the finest marble
His face curved on the finest terrazzo.
With the gravestone inscribed
"a lover, a mogul, parent and philanthropist."

For richer, for richer
I only mourn his passing for my children
But the funeral food was sweeter than my Christmas food.

Deep Seated

Methinks Uganda is a damned
And on the wheels of time,
Waiting for the hare not heir to take on...
He castigates the pen
As he glues closer to the golden stool of rule.

As many, genuflect for crumbs
To feed their glutton
The father secures and crowns son the crown prince
Awaiting ticking time.

The stole of rule,
Tamed by the Bachwezi.

Sihle Ntuli

Salvation

"There's really no such thing as the 'voiceless.' There are only the deliberately silenced, or the preferably unheard."
—Arundhati Roy

On the day of my baptism as a young
boy
I still recall blessed holy
water
washing over supple soft spot
of my head
baptism water inside my nose
pain right between the eyes.

& how did elders feel about salvation
I found myself asking the question
because on one day we would be
slaughtering
then on another day,

we would be praising the most high
during the pageantry of the black chuuch.

& so I posed the burning question
to a room full of elders while preparing
Sunday soul food of roast potatoes
& fried chicken

were we traditionalist or were we pious?

& whatever it was they were doing
they made it abundantly clear
that they had chosen not to hear me.

God Of Small Things

a villanelle

how will we learn to listen more?
& does life reveal our true purpose or are we too
naïve to notice the small things
how do I become more resilient?
how often should I pray in a single day?
in these moments you wonder
of the untenable commandments?
could it be possible to this pious or are we too
naïve to notice one small thing
in my difficulty to ask for forgiveness
the ease of placing the blame on my human nature
in these moments you wonder
how will we delay the masquerade?
how does one survive the carnival?
naïve to notice one small thing
is hope a song in sync with the hearts beating?
or a lone in the head voice slowing us down
& in these moments you wonder
of our naivety to notice the small things

The Saga (Concerning The Morning Call For Prayers)

one morning in the early hours
during the administering of Adhan ▨▨▨▨▨
while the sounds of the holy call emanated
from an Isipingo Mosque, one Hindu neighbour
restlessly turning in his bed, waiting
for the sun to show itself to him,
so he could begin the long journey
on his way to report the religious call to the law
there is a story told of a pharaoh
that once commissioned Haman
to build him a stone tower,
just so he could mount to the heavens
to wage war with the most high,
& towards this bold task, a dark cloud
of confounding confusion much like a normal person
attempting to speak in the language of the law
just as the infamous incident on the Tower of Babel,
a Hindu man, on one morning
rose from his bed, with a premeditation
to deflower the holy observation of Fajr r ▨▨▨▨ ▨▨▨▨▨
& by that evening on Al Jazeera
a report of the Hindu man on the court steps
celebrating his victory in a South African court of law,

a Durban high court judge ruling
that in the mornings, any sound emanating
from the Isipingo Mosque
is strictly prohibited from being heard anywhere
inside the Hindu man's house.

Gerry Sikazwe

Roots

Their hands planted and watered
The girth and length I now am

Their brains kneaded rare
thoughts
Into this tasty bread as wide as the
universe
Of humour, sweat, and hope
I served the world—
To be better, to reach further

Their words and prayers; advise
and wishes
Keep me warm and safe at night
In lonely valleys and threatening
high
Of dreams I chase, fresh paths I
tread

Yet always I grow distant
The further I fly, the farther I walk–

I have forgotten
The music of my father's voice
The hope on my mother's face

I am tired
Of being a tourist
In my parents' lives.

Worn Boldly And Gratefully

But as life has day and night
Mine too has faces
One of glittering smiles
And another of darkening frowns
One impressively witty
And another shamefully imbecilic
But as life has day and night
Proud of its fraternal twins
I too am not embarrassed of mine
I wear them boldly and gratefully
Knowing full well
That if not for them
The balance they shape
I would be a life mad and dangerous!

Single Tick

All it takes—
To live or to die
To heal or to hurt
To love or to betray
Is a single tick
Not its sound
Not five minutes
Not an hour
Or a lifetime.
All it takes—
Is a single tick.
Before its sound

Xitha Makgeta

P.O Box 16371

Like a dildo/ I dive in headfirst to swim with the sharks/
In a sea of currencies/ I'm paddling Rands/
Facing the current/ economic scale, inflation trends/
And the poor only have life to spend/
Its customer's custom to compare price/ cameras eye isles/
Sisters carry sold sign/ paypoint at the end of deep/
Where bills irritate sleep/ nightmares of month end/
We relate to the topic/ subscribe like reason money out logic/
The concept and its fabric/
Money power illusion, check book justice, credit card politics,
president plastic/
paralyzed budget, Johannesburg Stock Exchange figures of sorcery/
big companies' robbery/ they play us like toys/
Barbie in the consumers Pandora's Box, diagnosed shopaholics/
Living on credit/ still trying to sustain habits/
Poverty punch lines on comedy Calvary/
A carnival of capitalist, captains of industries play monopoly/
Wealthy families' oligopoly/
Trying to make it on the cover of Forbes Magazine/

Truth Is In The Vomit.

I'm stuck on a typewriter
Literary critic! I'm not the right (write) type
I brew a storm in a three-legged pot
Village vibes got my pen screeching rural thought
And granny bomb graffiti with cow dung
I stitch my tongue back in my mouth
Bushveldt riverbank free verse deposit
Breathing's hard with a smoke necklace
Bantustan episodes of Biko's ghost is Frank Talk
Kids fall in pit toilets and drown in faeces
Shock pumping like a communal water tap
Bring a bucket
Village tranquillity so moving it makes stomachs turn
And the truth is in the vomit.

It Is Blue In Harare

Harare streets will suck out the breath in you
What's worth a dollar when you can't breathe?
I autopilot across sidewalks
A traffic light with one eye robot itself
Police come out of the blue wagging batons like tails
Flip the coin it is the head of state
How quick the city loses its taste
Hurled into the fire's breathing
The burning that got Dzamara disappearing
I share a bench with Marechera's ghost at Unity Square
He spits poems in Shona, as if to d/train his tongue
There's fire in the streets
Prison walls eat us to the bone
We remain blue with a memory of stone

Ayouba Toure

A Song To The Fishes My Net Couldn't Hold

j.w
I bless you
for training my heart
for war
for making me believe
it's not every girl who prefers her lover black
and smart and whatever

e.w
I celebrate you
like the way a country celebrates its independence
like the way our house celebrated the conception
of a barren aunty
remember
in junior high you crawled into my chest
and grew into a burning desire
and for the first time in many years
I stopped cursing adam
for stupidly falling into a hole dug by an eve

k.s
like the man nailed to a cross
you are a god wearing human skin
once in an english class we are asked to describe
beauty and angel in one word
and I wrote your name.

Because We Are Made Up Of Water

the sea thinks of a reunion every time we walk out the door
of a clothing and swim into its arms when you enter a sea
chances are, you will fly into a ghost over time
the sea has registered more dead than the cemetery once
a young boy went to play beach soccer and bloomed into
a flower
inside the belly of the sea once in junior high our history
instructor wore the same clothes for days this man's
home
and belongings consumed the week before by a sea disease
once a party held on a beach transmogrified into a funeral after
the sea wrapped around bamba and squeezed him so tight that
he could fit inside a casket one time in the belly of a taxicab
in the belly of sinkor traffic in the belly of this shithole country
my phone yelled it's the news of a cousin erased by
the mediterranean throughout the remaining distance I paused
breathing and blinking a perfect way to save this city from flooding

from the ocean of mess that has gathered in my eyes
back home our house grew hoarse from screaming his
name

Liberia

After Allen Ginsberg
You have made breathing as tiring a thing as reaching
the last floor of the world's tallest building
by stairs. You have made survival as tedious as
swimming across the Atlantic. Your sun is merciless.
Your rain is cruel; it deprives us of our homes.
Your streets are flooded with bodies
that are not too far from rooting. At night,
the city becomes so dark that the moon screams
for mercy. It's two decades since the gun went off & still
Monrovia is obsessed with its black, thick smoke.
And still your soil keeps drinking our blood.
And still, everyone is running to the border. Liberia,
you pushed my cousin out of a speeding
Earth. He died because you couldn't secure him
what countries across the Mediterranean guarantee
their occupants: peace, skyscrapers, honey, roses,
education, pizza, shawarma, butterflies, moon,
snow, security. Liberia, when will you erase the holes
the bullets carved in our chests? When will you
anoint our stomachs? When will you turn our water
into wine? When will you allow us to be those birds,
partying in a perfect evening sky? Why
are the newspapers always like this—bleeding? Why is
every dream conceived under your sky a mountain?
Liberia, do you know the absence of rain that
makes us sunburn here is summer elsewhere? Liberia,
what the fuck are you waiting for to sing us to sleep?

Sarpong Osei Asamoah

A Boy Made Of Lines

Come, Yaro, off the blood walls of these bullet beaches.
These waters publish through you and break their sun spangled faces.
The bambino clouds are pink and yellow, and there's a village boy
transfixed by a river mirror in the moon cake of your teeth.
And I'm picking harmattan leaves off the ocean floor of repetition again.
Yaro, I'm gathering announcement cockerels' whistles for the cold again.
Inside my bones, a monsoon turns everything with clapping colours
into your mouth garden. I didn't start any of my life till I learned to bend
myself around the bed's jewellery. Come, Yaro, pledge our boat to
the Atlantic. Let's pretend till the blue line between us is rosewater.
Life is a naming game. Let's name the stone moon nipple of the night.
Yaro, let's offer our tongues twin names & watch them grow into
the couplets of your palm lines:
where the line breaks & my body begins.

The Rain & I

That October, the light that opened my teeth
was as yellow as the caramelised wings of Gabriel.
I touched you where I was sure to lose a finger.
I kissed the looming limbs of night, and it purred like a
full-bellied tiger,
sharpening his pyrotechnic teeth against a paralysed
appetite.
His smile was taffeta glass selfsame to God's sabertooth.
I was torn to shards as I rode the horns of dawn into the
tan future.
I was buried with the corpse of October.
If God cries in June and no one is around to tweet it,
does he have eyes?
That October, God blew his gun nose. And murdered
the rain & I.

Afrobeat

Who will survive in heaven
when Amerykans arrive there,
with their blood flowers, fallen towers
and shortened talons.
Who can escape their body
quicker than a bullet hole?
A blood-still body that inherits the leftover
palaces of silence.
Who will play the clarinet holes
in our faces when the drums
in the Kalashnikov kick off the afrobeat
& Europe pretends it cannot dance.

Caroline Anande Uliwa

Her Tabia (Habit)

Tease out the veins of Futility
From these Nipples

Allow the sacred frenzy | of their Hardening

Suss-out the earth where hope Seeds
Arrange this bed to my Unveiling
Manicured nails | gyrate her Butt

Evidence shares | you're a Ghost
While your lover snakes their Fingers
In your untamed Coils

Unfettered Tenderness
Lulling Hips

Moans unheard | escape your Lips

You Fight

But her hands mold skin too Right
Chasing the rancid | cocoa hues of my Legacy

Fingers celebrate | her Labia
We're coaxing out this tabia of Choosing

Self Defeat

*Tabia—Habit

Meeting Lonely

It's a lilac sky

Grey walls hint of sprouting palms

On a walk of epiphanies
Resolute fibres of my belly
Graceful muscles of my throat
Erode the burden of 'if only…'

In this journey of meeting lonely
Introspection behind face masks
Like bottles on a shooting range
They teeter and fall

Those excuses used to justify
Inequalities at our door
Gaps in the have & have not's
Necks strangled by authorities' norms

So I avoid the potholes
The rancid town planning
Focus on the splendid sunset

The indigenous green leaf
The meticulous effort by us all
To recover from our sores

Fast Phrases

Sun-bleached, white door curtain invites rest
To the hours spent on my butt now numb
Ducks waddling, defecating the backyard
Us on a mat, them centimetres apart

Eight hands are expertly pinching extensions to my scalp

A humble courtyard with five rooms
A commotion of tenants and the landlord 'Bibi Dina'
The entrance is to a sofa that's seen better days

Dilapidated by rain & dust, with stuff threatening to crumble its sides
Close by, a charcoal stove announces this is also the kitchen

The tree in the backyard speaks joy
There're spiels hidden in its feeble leaves
Latching on the frequency of boisterous gossip
Similar to the fast phrases now escaping lips
Of the ladies transforming my kinky afro coils

One of them Bibi Dina's daughter, Hawa
Feels like eating Ugali with sautéed greens

"Yani ukisha kaanga kitunguu,

tupia nyaya kwa mbali, usiiache mboga iive sana'

Her desire is pronounced with relish

As though speaking it alone allows her to savour the meal
As I huddled by four knee-covered 'dera' dresses
The 'wasusi' unveiled tales of their whole neighbourhood
Hawa's sister, who is becoming an alcoholic,
Stealing beer from that doctor's mistress
"Yani nashukuru mwanae ana tabia nzuri,
Yeye anaenda kanisani," Hawa adds.
Meanwhile, it felt like my head was having
An acupuncture gone horribly wrong

By night fall, my kinky coils were turned

Into a head full of lustrous braids in copper & golden hues
A Panadol had been doused for the headache
The commotions & vigour for life from that backyard
Allowed me to know & honour another facet

Of real African women

Ugali: A stiff porridge that's a traditional starch staple in Tanzania.

Adjei Agyei Baah

3 Senryū

Endtime Sermon

Bryan Rickert

long church service
praying for
its end

lady chews & pops gum
endtime sermon
fire and brimstone

the preacher's spittle
on the front row
after offering call

a congregant's bag
goes missing
an alter boy's pocket
bulging with bills

long sermon
a sleeper's fart
winds it up

Parting Through The Stars

I

drinks party
coming home
without my bike

II

drunk
I part through the stars
on my way home

III

homeward drunk
the wind rolls an empty can
after me

IV

waking up
from beer booze ⊠
this pee without end

V

morning light
my fart cuts through
the neighbourhood

Elec(sanc)tions

(To Africa & Her Elects)

I

political campaign
the peasants' anger
over his golden teeth

II

bursting at his seams
the politician tells us
to tighten our belts

III

seeking for our votes
the muddy trails left
by his campaigning car

IV

posing as a servant
the politician long waits
to speak to congregants

V

sworn in for the third time
the incumbent president wobbles
to take a seat

ACKNOWLEDGEMENTS.

A great many thanks to all those who made this book possible: especially my editor inchief for giving me the permission and the necessary resources to embark on thisproject, to each of the individual poets who trusted me with their work, to Tega and Evefor their immense support and strength throughout the whole project. And, to thecountless unnamedwhose wisdom, love, courage and resilience has been a hugeinspiration. This is an offering to the soul.

Henneh Kyereh Kwaku, *'Playing God in Old Love Skin, The Magician & Gaana'*,published in Lolwe. Copyright ©2020 Henneh Kyereh Kwaku. Used by permission of theauthor.

Gabriel Awauh Mainoo, *'7 shapes of God, A Dream Boy & A Black Skin Breaks AwayFrom Hell'*, from *Lyrical Textiles*. Copyright ©2021 Gabriel Awuah Mainoo. Reprintedby permission of the author.

Brian joe Okwesili, *'Preacher Man Knows My name,'* appeared in Icefloe Press 2021,*'My Prayers Do Not Promise Me Heaven,'* appeared in Praxis Mag Online 2021; *'HeHatched into a Howl'*, appeared in Isele Magazine 2021. Copyright ©2021 Brian JoeOkwesili. Used by permission of the author.

Christine Coates, *'Threnody for a queen in four parts– an opera'*, *'The CollapsedMother'* & *'Tears for Medusa'*, from *The Summer We Didn't Die.* Copyright©2020.Christine Coates. Reprinted by the permission of the author.

Jeremy Teddy Karn, 'Portrait of a Liberian Boy, Sickle Cell Anemia & The Making of Grief', appeared in Lolwe. Copyright © 2020. Jeremy Teddy Karn. Used by permission of the author.

Amirah Al Wassif, *'Human Tragedy, Diaries of Jail'*, appeared in *Academy of Heart and Mind Journal*; *'Hallucinations'*, appeared in *Silver Blade Magazine*. Copyright

©2021 Amirah Al Wassif. Used by permission of the author.

Nondwe Mpuma, *'History of the Year'*, appeared in *Peach Country*. Copyright ©2022 Nondwe Mpuma. Used by permission of the author.

Londeka Mdluli, *'The sky has robbers',* appeared in Prometheusdreaming(www.prometheusdreaming.com), *'Immigration',* appeared in *The Spectacle Magazine*;*'Pigeon Houses'.* Copyright ©2020, 2021, 2021 Londeka Mdluli. Used by permission of the author.

Timothy Fab-Eme, *'We're Sick Now and Earth is Healing Real Fast'*, appeared in *NewFeathers Anthology*: edited by Fox Chapman and O'Leary. Copyright ©2020 TimothyFab Eme. Reprinted with permission from the author.

Nebeolisa Okwudili, *'The Making of Widows'*, appeared in *Threepenny Review*.Copyright ©2017 Nebeolisa Okwudili. Used by permission of the author. Pusetho Lame,*'Botswana, Thoughts & Dear Death'*, from *Ocean of Untold Goodbyes*. Copyright ©2019Lame Pusetso. Reprinted by permission of the author.

Nsah Mala, *'Forbidden, Sometimes I Wonder, & Cloudy Days'*, from *Bites of Insanity*.Copyright ©2015 Nsah Mala. Reprinted by permission of the author.

Erasto E. Noni, '*Song ofBeauty, Africa, My Africa & The Sleeping Bees*', from TheTropicalSongs.Copyright©2017ErastoE.Noni. Reprintedbypermissionoftheauthor.

Billyhadiat T. Adeola, *'Paradise in between my legs, This is not love & HoneymoonBlues',* from *DECEMBER BEGINS THE NEW YEAR.* Copyright © 2020 BillyhadiatTaofeeqoh Adeola. Used by permission of the author.

Nnane Ntube, *'Magical Pen, The Wait & Nothing Like a Kiss'*, appeared in SpillwordsPress. Copyright ©2017, 2021, 2022 Nnane Ntube. Used by permission of the author.

Phalani A. Nyoni, *'LXXIV, CLI & CCLV'*, from *Mars His Sword*. Copyright ©2018 Philani A. Nyoni. Reprinted by permission of the author.

Hauwa Shaffili Nuhu, *'Fault lines, Prayer & Praying'*, from 'Sister'. Copyright ©2021 Hauwa Shaffili Nunu. Reprinted by permission of the author.

Sihle Ntuli, 'Salvation', appears in Bayou Review. Copyright ©2022 Sihle Ntuli. Used by permission of the author.

Gerry Sikazwe, *'Worn Boldly and Gratefully, Single Tick & Roots'*, appeared in Spillwords Press, Writers Space Africa and Ake Review, respectively. Copyright ©2018, 2020, 2021 Gerry Sikazwe. Used by permission of the author.

Xitha Makgeta, *'It is blue in Harare'*, appeared in *Poetry Potion*. Copyright ©2022 Xitha Makgeta. Used with permission from the author.

Youba Toure, *'A Song to All The Fishes My Net Couldn't Hold, Because We are Made Up of Water & Liberia'*, appeared in *Olongo Africa, Lolwe & IcwFlore Press*, respectively. Copyright 2021, 2021, 2022 Youba Toure. Used with permission from the author.

Adjei Agyei-Baah, 'Endtime Sermon, Parting through the stars & Ele(sanc)tions, appeared in *Failed Haiku Journal*. Copyright ©2021 Adjei Agyei-Baah. Used with the permission of the author.

Contributors Biographical Notes

Henneh K. Kwaku is a poet of Bono heritage and the author of *'Revolution of the Scavengers'* (African Poetry BookFund/Akashic Books, 2020). A 2022 resident at the Library of Africa and the African Diaspora, and the host/Rev of The Church of Poetry. He is originally from Gonasua in the Jaman South Municipality (Bono Region) of Ghana. His work has appeared in Academy of American Poets' A-Poem-A-Day, World Literature Today, Lolwe and elsewhere. He tweets @Kwaku_kyereh.

Gabriel A. Mainoo is a Ghanaian writer, poet, editor and lyricist. Winner of the Singapore Poetry Prize, Africa Haiku Prize, a LFP/ RML/ Library of Africa and the African Diaspora Chapbook winner. He pursues tertiary education at the University of Cape Coast and is a recipient of the West Africa Writers Residency. He is an author of five books, and *'Sea Ballet'* forthcoming. Gabriel is a tennis professional in the morning, a student in the afternoon, and a writer in the evening.

Ruvimbo C. Chikanda (Rubzi) is a 20 year old zimbabwean poet, spoken word artist, and storyteller. Her passion for the arts began when she realised that words were the best route of expression for her. As a child, she lived and breathed arts and culture; writing, reciting and performing became her daily bread. The issues within community and experiences in her day to day life make up a greater part of her creations. Ruvimbo manages to speak for the voiceless and be a beacon that helps bring attention to the pressing situations taking place around, and in a comical manner at times.

Brian Joe Okwesili is a queer Nigerian poet and storyteller. His works explore the interiority and tensions of queerness in a heteronormative culture in which he imagines a world of inclusivity. His works appear in *CRAFT, SLICE, Smokelong Quarterly, Isele Magazine, Foglifter, Tupelo Quarterly, Brittle Paper, PANK,* and elsewhere. He is currently a student of law at the University of Calabar, Cross River State, Nigeria.

Cristine Coates is a poet from Cape Town, South Africa. She has an M.A. (Creative Writing) from the University of Cape Town. Her debut collection *'Homegrown'* (Modjaji Books 2014) received an honourable mention from the Glenna Luschei Prize. *'FIRE DROUGHT WATER'*, was published by Damselfly Books, 2018, and *'The Summer We Didn't Die'* by Modjaji Books, 2020. Coates is sensitive to environmental issues, finds solace and inspiration in nature. She also has an interest in life-writing and the recovery of personal history through public and private imagery.

Kwaku Dade began writing poetry as a teenager and has several poems aired on the *Writers Project of Ghana* radio program, as well contributing to the *Best 'New' African Poets Anthology* (Mwanaka Publishing 2017). He created and directed a play commemorating the United Nations' 75TH anniversary in Ghana in 2020. Since 2016, he has focused on developing his distinct voice, which celebrates the resilience of the human spirit.

Jeremy Teddy Karn's chapbook, 'Miryam Magdalit', was selected by Kwame Dawes and Chris Abani for the New Generation African Poet (African Book Fund, 2021). His works have appeared and are forthcoming in *Olney Magazine, Penn Review, Hoxie Gorge Review, Ghost heart literary Journal, Whale Road, IceFloe Press, Lolwe, Up the Staircase Quarterly* and elsewhere. He is the 2020 winner of the ARTmosterrific editor choice award. He tweets @jeremy_karn96

Phodiso Modirwa is a Mostwana writer and poet with works published in *Brittle Paper, Lolwe, 20.35 Africa: An Anthology of Contemporary Poetry, Jalada Africa, The Weight Of Years: An Afroanthology of Creative Nonfiction* and elsewhere. She is a recipient of the Botswana President's Award- Contemporary Poetry 2016 and recently completed her poetry residency at the Gaborone Art Residency Centre in Gaborone, Botswana. She is the author of the Chapbook, '*Speaking In Code*' included New Generation African Poets: A Chapbook Boxset (Tisa).

Taofeek Ayeyemi 'Aswagaaway' is a Nigerian lawyer, writer and the author of four chapbooks, including 'Tongueless Secrets' (Ethel Press, 2021) and a full length collection 'aubade at night or serenade in the morning' (Flowersong Press, 2021). A BotN and Pushcart Prize nominee, his works have appeared in *Contemporary Verse 2, Lucent Dreaming, Up-the-Staircase Quarterly, FERAL, Frogpond, Modern Haiku* and elsewhere. He won the 2021 Loft Books Flash Fiction Competition, 2nd place in the 2021 Porter House Review Poetry Contest, and Honourable mention in the 2021 Ito En Oi Ocha Shin-Haiku Contest, 2021 Oku-no-hosomichi Soka Matsubara Haiku Contest, and 2020 Stephen A. DiBiase Poetry Prize among others. He tweets @Aswagaawy

Alvin Kathembe is a writer from Nairobi, Kenya. His poetry has been featured in Dust *Poetry Magazine, The Short Story Foundation Journal, Poetry Potion,* and other publications. He co-edited *Down The River Road's* third issue– *'Asphyxia'*. His short stories have been published in *Jalada, Omenana, Brittle Paper,* and *Equipoise* available on Kindle. He tweets @SofaPhilosopher.

Amirah Al Wassif is an Egyptian poet and writer. She is the author of five books in Arabic and two in English, including a poetry collection titled 'For Those Who Don't Know Chocolate', and 'The Cocoa Boy and Other Stories'. Amirah has her work widely published in various magazines and journals worldwide. Her work has been translated into Spanish, Kurdish, Hindi and Arabic.

Nondwe Mpuma was born eMaXesibeni in the Eastern Cape province. She holds an MA Creative Writing from the University of Western Cape, and is currently a lecturer at the same institution. She is the winner of the 2017 Patricia Schonstein Poetry in Mcgregor Award and has been published widely in South Africa, and abroad. She is one of the hosts of the The Red Wheelbarrow Society based in Cape Town. She writes because she loves to read and wants to be able to imagine someone like herself and those she knows in what she reads.

Prince R. Chidzvondo is an award winning and NAMA certified writer, content creator, media practitioner, and artist outspoken, hearty and real. Performing under Moonchild Rye, the Harare based writer is driven to create, grow and impact with memorability and uniqueness. He presents a new generation of storytelling that is authentic and deliberately competitive in a world that demands bold and daring creativity. '*Under My Skin*' (2018) is his first published collection of poetry.

Londeka Mdluli is a South African born writer and storyteller. She was born in South Africa, but does not shy away from her Zimbabwen heritage. She is currently pursuing a degree in Library Science and Philosophy at the University of Western Cape, in Cape Town. Mdluli began writing at the age of 9 after falling in love with rhetoric, she has since written many of her pieces based on what she finds most charming.

Richard Mbuthia is a teacher, poet, motivational speaker and editor. He has been teaching English to children aged between 8 and 15 for over twenty years, in Kenya and Tanzania. He is passionate about helping to inculcate and develop the poetic craft in children. He is also a published poet in books, magazines and on different online forums and outlets.

Timothy Fab-Eme is an engineer and a poet interested in environmental and social justice. He is the issue 7 editor of Reckoning: Creative Writing on Environmental Justice; a recipient of Cove Park Residencies on Climate Action, and a poetry MFA candidate at the University of Notre Dame. Tim loves exploring the wonders of Nature, gardening, and fishing in the mangrove swamps of his island home, Egun-Okom (Ogonokom). His work has appeared in *The Malahat Review, New Welsh Review, FIYAH, Delmarva Review, apt, Reckoning*, and *Magma*.

Nebeolisa Okwudili is a Nigerian writer whose poems have appeared in the Threepenny Review, *The Sewanee Review, The Cincinnati Review, Salamander Magazine, Beloit Poetry Journal*, and are forthcoming in *Image Journal*. His nonfiction has appeared in *Catapult* and *CommonWealth Writers*. He is an MFA student of the Iowa Writers Workshop, where he was awarded a Provost Fellowship and won the Prairie Lights John Leggetts Prize for Fiction. He was also a finalist (first runner up) for the Granum Foundation Fellowship Prize.

Leroy Mtulisi Ndlovu is a writer from Bulawayo, Zimbabwe. He loves to write stories about his life and those around him. He is the author of *'Tales of Youth and Love'*. He is also an actor. He won Best Actor at the 2021 Bulawayo Arts Awards for his performance in *'Figure it Out'*, and is a member of the cast of TV shows such as *VIVA Wenera*, and *Amanxeba*.

Pusetho Lame is a 25 year old multi award winning poet, a spoken word artist and motivational speaker from Hukuntsi, in Kgalagadi North in Botswana. She is the author of 11 books. She has earned herself the name 'Poeticblood' through her outstanding and sterling work in the creative industry and winning spoken word performances both locally and internationally. Pusetso is also the Managing Director of an award winning publishing company Poeticblood publishers, she has over the years made an impact both locally and internationally through her writing skills by raising young authors and publishing over 150 books. She is a registered member of the National Writers Association of South Africa and the Botswana ambassador of the African Writers Round Table.

Nsah Mala is a poet, writer, editor, translator and literary scholar from Mbesa (Mbessa) in Cameroon, writing in Mbessa, English and French. An alumnus of the Caine Prize Workshop, he has published five collections of poetry, and four picture books. He won the Ministry of Arts and culture Short Story Prize (Cameroon) in 2006 and the 2017 Prix Litteraire Malraux (France) for poetry in French. Life and its challenges inspire him.

Isaac Kwaliba is a lover of art from Kenya. He writes and reads poetry, creative nonfiction and fiction. His work has been published in Scotland's Driech Magazine's Wee Book of Wee Poetry, The Kalahari Reviews, The Kenya Studies Review and The Best 'New' African Poets anthology (Mwanaka Publishing, 2020) His work is inspired by everyday life experiences and the observation of the complexities of human nature in relation to philosophy and religion.

Nehemiah Omukhonya is a Kenyan poet who loves having fun with words. He writes in Kiswahili and English, and derives his inspiration from daily life activities. His works have been published online across various platforms, including *Writers Space Africa* and *Poetry Soup*.

Mukonya was on the shortlist for the 2019 Wakini Kuria Award for Children's Literature. He currently serves as the national coordinator for Writers Space Africa Kenya.

Ann Pendo Njeri is a blogger, teacher, poet, and writer. From a young age selling at her mom's kiosk books were her only friends. The pen became her voice and paper her rhythm. She has learned to translate her emotions through melodious wordplay.She will definitely write what she feels.

Erasto E. Noni is a degree holder, professional teacher, and an author of literary works particularly novels and poems. Erasto is inspired by nature like mountains, flowers, grass and water, adventures and life experience. He co-authored a poetry anthology *'The Tropical Songs'* (2017), published a Swahili novel *'Jasho La Mvua'* (2021).

Energy Mavaza, also known by the stage name Poyetik Enej, a page and spoken word poet, an author and sports writer in all. Was born on the 27th of November 1990 in Harare. His poetry journey was ignited at Induna High School in Bulawayo when he stumbled across the poetic artistry of Wilfred Owen who died at the young age of 27 but whose war-time experience is encoded through poetry. He has authored a poetry anthology titled *Beneath the African Sun* and a Novel titled *The Undaunting Spirit.*

Aisha N. Ahmad

Carolyne M. Acen (Afroetry MA) is a Ugandan poet, spoken word artist, author and activist whose works mostly revolve around women stories. She currently manages Eco minds Poets, a group of 9 female poets dedicated to bringing women's stories to the stage in a theatrical production. She is also the Vice President of the Poets Association of Uganda. in 2021, she was nominated for the Janzi Awards under Outstanding Spoken Word.

Tryphena Yeboah is a Ghanaian writer and the author of the poetry chapbook '*A Mouthful of Home*', selected for the New African Generation Poets Series. Her fiction and essays have appeared in *Narrative Magazine, CommonWealth Writers, and Lit Hub*, among others. She is currently a Ph.D. student at the University of Nebraska-Lincoln, studying English with an emphasis in Creative Writing.

Ronald K. Ssekajja is a realist, a technologist, and a poet. He is the author of *'Echoes of Tired Men', 'Dancing on Broken Lines', 'Footsteps of the Kakalabanda', 'Wet Lips', 'When Dreams Die',* and *'Olwendo Ly' Ebiyiiye'* and currently working on launching *'The Renaissance'* and *'Needles & Hospital Bedsheet'* all poetry collections. He draws inspiration from Art, Photography, and the struggles of human life.

Jeresi Katusiime is a writer, a boy mom, and a networking assistant during the day. She writes screenplays, film scripts, poetry, and stories that wont let her sleep before they are out of her head. She loves sunsets and photography. And, she accords all her creativity to God.

Carla-Ann Makumbe is a poet, and aspiring novelist. She is the author of *'And To Patricia I Had To Man Up'*. Carla-Ann derives her inspiration from society and she is always willing to tackle issues most whisper about.

Jasper H. Sabuni (Kido) is a Tanzanian poet, writer, social justice activist and a spoken word artist, who has performed his poetry on different platforms in Tanzania, South Africa and Brazil, known as, 'Kido' his stage name. He is passionate about poetry and literature in general. He uses his artistry as his medium of disseminating knowledge, raising consciousness, spreading love and hope. He is the author of the bilingual (English-Swahili) poetry collection *'Love Chronicles'*.

Nicole N. Chimanikire is a poetic mind that dabbles in the creation of art, as a form of youth advocacy for children and youth rights but also as an expression of her day to day living as a Zimbabwean girl. She is an individual who takes pride in her heritage and African descent. Overarching poetic themes ranging from poetry of introspection, Gender based violence, mental health, and SRHR issues. Believing. All rooted in the belief of poetry from the soul, for the soul.

Justine Nagundi is a Ugandan writer published in midnight & indigo; a platform for black female writers, and in Writers Space Africa. She is also a stage actress with the Footlights Playhouse in Uganda. Her poetry is inspired by the need to be understood by every lover of words. She is a member of Stubborn Poetry, a poetry label in Uganda.

Fungai G. Makuyana is a mother, wife, tv presenter, entrepreneur and writer and raised in Zimbabwe with the glory of a Rozvi Princess. She is a unique voice, expressing her cries over the struggles of Black women in society, Her writing conjures up an eclectic, even eccentric image through the diverse collection of endeavours she experienced in her young life and delivers these with melancholy and stubble rage. When she is not reading or. writing. She spends her time with loved ones, travelling, cooking and learning new skills. She believes that poetry can change the world, and she uses it to inspire and empower young people through writing.

Elizabeth K. Lukoma is a procurement officer who fell in love with words as a young girl listening to her father read stories to her and the siblings every night before bed. She was born in the beautiful hills of Kabale in the South Western part of Uganda and is married to an amazing man. Her inspiration stems from the experiences of her daily life, and a need to echo those who have not been heard.

Emestina E. Azah loves time bending movies and a good nap, enjoys long walks and listening to podcasts from On Being Studios. She has work published by Agbowo, Tampered Press and Writers Space Africa.

Tatiana N. Kondo (Banshee) is a groundbreaking award winning spoken word artist who uses her rhetoric to promote creative advocacy. She is also a creative entrepreneur who is in the business of hosting, planning and curating events, story telling, proofreading and editing. She is the founder of the Shee movement and spearheads the annual Battle scars and Healing event which encourages mental wellness through the arts.

Oppong C. Benjamin's collection of poems, *'Collecting Stars From A Night's Sky'* (Poetic Justice Books & Arts, 2019) won the 3rd prize in the prestigious Professor Atukwei Okai Poetry Prize in 2019. He is also the author of a short story collection *'The Virgin Mother and Other Short Stories'* (Forte Monrovia, 2017). He has read his work at literary events in Ghana, Nigeria, South Africa, Liberia, Rwanda, German, Norway, and Russia.

Billyhadiat T. Adeola is a mandala artist, poet and author of the chapbook *'December Begins The New Year'* (WWR Chapbook Series, 2020). She is a lover of patterns, shapes, and components, which she attempts to speak into words with poetry. Her poetry theme(s) are where grief and love console each other, where birth and death pat each other's backs. She is a contributor to *African Writers*, she was shortlisted for PIN's Poetically Written Prose. She writes from the golden-rust city of Ibadan.

Nnane Ntube is a poet from Cameroon. She is a literary activist with a good understanding of proactive reading techniques. Nnane has authored a poetry collection titled *'Litany of a Foreign Wife'* (Spears Media Press, 2020). She currently serves as an assistant editor at *Poetic Africa Magazine*. She is a recipient of the Sub Sahara Advisory Panel (SSAP) grant for artists and writers under the Madaraja Project.

Philani A. Nyoni born in Zimbabwe, he is an awards winning author of books including *'Once A Lover Always A Fool'* (2012), *'Hewn From Rock'* (2014) with John Eppel, *'Philtrum'* (2017). He also published in two international anthologies: *'Splinters Of A Mirage Dawn'* (2017), and *'The Gonjun Pin and Other Stories'*. He is a world record holding sonneteer. His poetry was used in narrating the award winning short film 'Jane The Ghost'. His short story *'Celestial Incest'* was short listed for the African Writers' Awards in 2018.

Hauwa S. Nuhu is a poet and an essayist from Nigeria, with work published on *African Arguments, Popula, Jalada Africa, The Republic* and elsewhere. She's a 2018 fellow of the Ebedi Writers Residency, a 2021 Bada Murya Fellow, and a 2022 Storify Africa fellow. She currently works as a journalist with *HumAngle*, covering displacement and migration.

Esnala Banda is an award winning writer, poet, marketer and photographer. She is passionate about the real stories and representation of African humanity, she looks to keep exploring the human condition most especially from an African perspective; to explore through her work the nuances of African human emotion and existence and translating that into something relatable and wholesome.

Zziwa Zinbala is an affiliate with the Stubborn Poetry group in Uganda. He has interests in poetic drama, his debut poetic play, *'The Muchwezi, The Flower & The Suitor'* comes out in 2023 he writes in his home country Uganda.

Sihle Ntuli is a poet and classicist from Durban, South Africa, he has had work published in notable publications such as *The Rumpus, SAND journal, Transition Magazine, and ANMLY*. He is the author of *'Rublin'* (uHlanga, 2020). His work is inspired by everyday life. He is extremely passionate about the page poetry scene from the African continent more especially because of the huge strides that have been made over the past few years.

Gerry Sikazwe is a Lusaka, based Zambian writer and poet. He is the author of the poetry collections, *'Words That Matter'* (Mwanaka Publishers, 2018), AMD *'Take Me With You'* (2020, Nib Hub Books). His third poetry collection, *'Here Is A Painting'* is forthcoming is 2022.

Xitha Mkgeta is a South African, Pretoria based writer, performer and art activist. He's the founder and facilitator of the Writeusanonymous poetry program running at the Stanza Bopape Library. He's a former ambassador of the UNISA Poetry Society. He is the author of a poetry chapbook titled *'Bits & Pieces'* (2016) and studio (EP) *'In Fragments'* (2008) *'Rap- Oetree'* (2010). He has toured and performed on different stages locally and internationally including, Split This Rock Poetry Festival (USA), Harare Literary Festival (ZIM), Grahamstown National Arts Festival.

Ayouba Toure, a pushcart nominee, writes from Paynesville, Liberia. He is a student of Dr. Patricia Jabbeh Wesley and co-founder of Pepper Coast Lit. His work has been published or forthcoming in *Lolwe, Olongo Africa, Olney Magazine, IceFlore Press, Cutthroat Magazine* and elsewhere.

Sarpong O. Asamoah is a bilingual Ghanaian writer living in Accra, Ghana. He is the founding member of the Contemporary Ghanaian Writers Series (CGWS). He has also been an intern at the Library Of Africa and The African Diaspora (LOATAD). His work has been featured *in Tampered Press Magazine, Porotrean, Agbowo Magazine, Lolwe* and elsewhere. *These poems (In this collection) are artefacts of my self discovery. They came as testament to my need to explore the evidence of my identity as a function of my existence. They are also – in 'afrobeat' –an attempt to sing of the existence, history and identity of Africa.*

Caroline A. Uliwa is a native of Tanzania with ancestors coming mostly from the foothills of Kilimanjaro. She articulates the complexities of human actions/emotions with words and melody, as a singer/poet and a budding percussionist. Her genre of music is 'Spoken Word-Afro-Jazz'. She likes working with live musicians and so she has worked with an eclectic bunch from experienced guitarists, bassists to Cello players, beat boxers, Cajun players and percussionists. Caroline has been featured regularly in various entertainment platforms in the city including Soma Book Cafe, Poetry 255, Lyricist Lounge, Chi & Friends. In 2017 she released her own music in a live concert at Soma Book Cafe.

Adjei Agyei Baah is a lecturer, translator, editor and currently a PhD student at the University of Waikato, New Zealand. He is the co-founder of Africa Haiku Network, and *The Mamba*, Africa's first international haiku journal. Adjei is a globally anthologised poet and proponent of Afriku, a nativized form of the Japanese haiku poetry. His debut haiku collection, *AFRIKU* (Red Moon Press, 2016), has been praised by Africa's first Nobel Prize laureate, Wole Soyinka, Adjei is the author of six poetry collections, which were largely influenced by his African surroundings.

About The Editor:

Nyashadzashe Chikumbu better known as ***Svovanepasi*** , his ancestral family name is a poet, writer, editor and a political analyst. He is a columnist *for The Migrant Online*, and *Review and Mail*, he is a trustee of the African Writers Development Trust, an arts NGO with its headquarters in Nigeria, that seeks to empower African writers. He sat on the panel of judges for the 2018 African Writers Award. He was one of 3 keynote poets at the Unesco Refugee Integration through Languages and the Arts (RILA) Spring School 2022 at the University of Glasgow, Scotland.

CPSIA information can be obtained
at www.ICGtesting.com
Printed in the USA
BVHW071109020822
643543BV00010B/1087